PRAYER IN
THE CATHOLIC
TRADITION

A Symposium With
Dianne Bergant, C.S.A., Susan A. Calef, Ph.D.,
Very Reverend Gregory Polan, O.S.B.,
Mary Collins, O.S.B., Elizabeth A. Dreyer, Ph.D.,
Most Reverend Raymond J. Boland, D.D.

Edited by Richard W. Miller II, Ph.D.

Liguori

LIGUORI, MISSOURI

Imprimi Potest:
Thomas D. Picton, C.Ss.R.
Provincial, Denver Province
The Redemptorists

ISBN 978-0-7648-1597-3
© 2007, Catholic Community Foundation of Kansas City
Library of Congress Catalog Card Number: 2007921462
Printed in the United States of America
11 10 09 08 07   5 4 3 2 1

All rights reserved. No part of this publication may be reproduced, stored in a retrieval system, or transmitted in any form or by any means—electronic, mechanical, photocopy, recording, or any other—except for brief quotations in printed reviews, without the prior permission of the publisher.

Scripture citations are taken from the *New Revised Standard Version of the Bible*, copyright 1989 by the Division of Christian Education of the National Council of the Churches of Christ in the USA. All rights reserved. Used with permission.

Selected Scripture quotations are taken from the *New American Bible*, copyright © 1970, 1986, 1991 by the Confraternity of Christian Doctrine, 3211 Fourth Street, N.E., Washington, DC 20017-1194, and are used with permission. All rights reserved.

Excerpt from *Deus Caritas Est*, Pope Benedict XVI, copyright © 2005, Libreria Editrice Vaticana. All rights reserved. Used with permission.

Excerpt from *The Art of Passing Over: An Invitation to the Art of Living Creatively*, copyright © 1988 by Francis Dorff. All rights reserved. Used with permission of Paulist Press, www.paulistpress.com.

Liguori Publications, a nonprofit corporation, is an apostolate of the Redemptorists. To learn more about the Redemptorists, visit *Redemptorists.com.*

To order, call 1-800-325-9521
www.liguori.org

Contents

Appendix I ~ 113
A Sampling of Written Questions Presented at the Symposium

Appendix II ~ 115
Speakers' Biographies

Introduction

*Richard W. Miller II, Ph.D., Assistant Professor of
Systematic Theology, Creighton University*

At last year's conference, we addressed a current phenomenon
in the United States of people identifying themselves as "spiritual, but not religious." This common self-identification suggests
that religious traditions and communities are considered, at best,
irrelevant and, at worst, detrimental to one's spiritual life. We responded to this sentiment by clarifying the connection between the
central mysteries and doctrines of the faith and the spiritual lives of
Christians.[1] This year's conference on "Prayer in the Catholic Tradition" complements last year's conference on spirituality; indeed, it
completes what we began last year: Prayer is the foundation of the
spiritual life. Prayer is, according to Romano Guardini, "as necessary
to a human being's spiritual existence as the laws of logic are to his
intellectual life or the spatial order is to his physical existence."[2]

In the few minutes available to me I would like to draw your
attention to the relationship between doctrine and prayer. While it
is important to recognize, as we did in last year's conference, that the
doctrines of Christianity inform an authentic Christian spirituality,
it is also important to understand that in the history of the Christian

---

1. See Richard W. Miller II, ed., *Spirituality for the 21st Century: Experiencing God in
the Catholic Tradition* (Liguori, Missouri: Liguori Publications, 2006).

2. Romano Guardini, *The Art of Praying: The Principles and Methods of Christian Prayer,*
formerly entitled *Prayer in Practice*, trans. Prince Leopold of Loewenstein-Wertheim
(New York: Pantheon Books, 1957, 1985; reprinted, Manchester, New Hampshire: So-
phia Institute Press, 1994), p. 54. Here Guardini is particularly stressing the prayer of
adoration. In addition, I have slightly changed the quotation to use inclusive language.
The English translation reads "as necessary to man's spiritual existence as the laws of
logic are to his intellectual life or the spatial order is to his physical existence."

tradition the prayer life of the community has played an important role in the debates leading to the formation of doctrines. The idea that prayer informs doctrine was explicitly articulated in the fifth century by Prosper of Aquitaine in his Latin formula *lex orandi, lex credendi*, which can be translated as "the law of prayer is the law of belief." Reviewing the employment of this axiom in the whole history of the development of doctrine is beyond the scope of this brief introduction. It is, however, instructive to point out that although the often quoted formula *lex orandi, lex credendi* was articulated in the fifth century, the idea that prayer indicates what we believe was employed prior to the fifth century. In fact, it was an idea that was important in the debates leading to the formation of the central doctrine of the faith, namely, the doctrine of the Trinity.

The development of the doctrine of the Trinity began with the question of whether or not Christ was God. Reflection upon this question reached its climax in the Arian Controversy of the fourth century. Arius held that Christ was merely a creature. The Council of Nicaea in 325 and its great defender, Athanasius, held that Christ was truly God. Among the barrage of arguments that Athanasius leveled against the Arians was the argument that our prayer indicates what we believe. Athanasius maintained that both Scripture and the prayers of the community suggest that Christ is to be worshipped. And if God alone is worthy of worship, then Christ must be God.

After the divinity of Christ was generally accepted in the 360s, the question of whether or not the Holy Spirit was God came to the fore. In the debates concerning the divinity of the Holy Spirit, the argument that our prayers indicate what we believe exercised an even greater influence. One of Athanasius' arguments was again in this vein. In particular, he maintained that the Holy Spirit is God because in the prayer at baptism, which is taken from the great commission in Matthew's Gospel (Matthew 28:19), we are baptized in the name of the Father, and of the Son, and of the Holy Spirit.

The argument from prayer became even more significant for

Basil of Caesarea, one of the great Cappadocian theologians and a doctor of the Church. Basil did not think the evidence from Scripture was strong enough to maintain that the Holy Spirit, like the Son, was a distinct person within the Godhead.[3] Hence, Basil turned to the prayer of the Christian community as affirmation of the divinity of the Spirit. In his enormously influential treatise *On the Holy Spirit*, Basil analyzed the prayers of the community as evidence for right Christian belief. He viewed the prayers of the community as part of the oral tradition that had been passed down from the apostles. As such, for Basil, the prayers of the Church were authoritative in matters of doctrine.

While Basil, like Athanasius, appealed to the Matthean baptismal formula, he also pointed to the use of two doxologies in worship as evidence for the divinity of the Spirit.[4] The first doxology was "Glory to the Father through the Son in the Holy Spirit." It was the customary formula for the Greek-speaking Church at the time.[5] By using the preposition *in,* the first doxology, according to Basil, "expresses the relationship between ourselves and the Spirit,"[6] and thus "describes the grace we have been given."[7] The second doxology was "Glory be to the Father with the Son together with the Holy Spirit." This doxology was the customary formula of the Churches in the East that did not speak Greek.[8] The preposition *with*, for Basil, indicated that the Spirit is a distinct person in God and is eternally united in communion with God. The underlying assumption of

---

3. See the magisterial work of R.P.C. Hanson, *The Search for the Christian Doctrine of God: The Arian Controversy 318–381*(Edinburgh: T&T Clark, 1988), 777.

4. Doxologies are words of praise to God that conclude liturgical prayers.

5. David Anderson, introduction to *On the Holy Spirit*, by Saint Basil the Great, trans. David Anderson (Crestwood, NY: St. Vladimir's Seminary Press), 11.

6. Saint Basil the Great, *On the Holy Spirit*, trans. David Anderson (Crestwood, NY: St. Vladimir's Seminary Press), Ch. 27 paragraph 68; p. 102.

7. Ibid.

8. Anderson, introduction to *On the Holy Spirit*, 11.

Basil's rather sophisticated analysis was that the content of the community's prayers revealed the content of their belief.

In the Creed defined at the Council of Nicaea in 325, the Holy Spirit barely got a walk-on role. Nicaea was concerned with the establishment of the divinity of the Son in response to the Arians. Thus the Creed of Nicaea spends a paragraph refuting Arianism and enumerating the characteristics of the Son that show that the Son is truly God. Conversely, the Creed of Nicaea only states belief in the Holy Spirit without further elaborating on the status and characteristics of the Spirit. More than fifty years later, however, after much controversy and debate, and in large part due to the efforts of Basil and the other Cappadocian fathers (Gregory of Nazianzus and Gregory of Nyssa), the Council of Constantinople, in 381 issued a much fuller statement concerning the Holy Spirit. The Creed from the Council of Constantinople essentially affirmed the Creed of Nicaea and expanded upon the teaching on the Holy Spirit such that the Creed from the Council of Constantinople is often called the Nicene-Constantinopolitan Creed. In fact, the Creed that we profess as Roman Catholics during Sunday Mass and that is popularly known as the Nicene Creed is really the Creed issued at the Council of Constantinople with the later addition of the *filioque* clause.[9]

---

9. The Creed from the Council of Constantinople maintains that the Holy Spirit proceeds from the Father. The so-called Nicene Creed said by Roman Catholics today at Sunday Mass states that the Holy Spirit "proceeds from the Father and the Son." This addition of "and the Son" is the *filioque* clause because *filioque* in Latin means "and the Son." The idea that the Son has a role in the origin of the Holy Spirit was a matter of dispute as early as the fourth century, but it was not until the sixth century that it is found in the profession of faith of the Third Council of Toledo (589) and until the eleventh century that it is introduced into the Roman liturgy of the Mass by Pope Benedict VIII (d. 1024). The Eastern Christian Churches strongly disagreed with this unilateral addition to the Nicene-Constantinopolitan Creed by the West so much so that it was a contributing factor to the schism between the Eastern and Western Churches in the eleventh century.

In the creedal definition at Constantinople we can see the traces of Basil's argument from worship. After the sections expressing belief in the Father and the Son, the Creed turns to belief in the Holy Spirit and it says, "…[We believe] in the Holy Spirit, the Lord and life-giver, Who proceeds from the Father, Who with the Father and the Son is *together worshipped and together glorified*, Who spoke through the prophets."[10]

By affirming that the Holy Spirit is to be worshipped together with the Father and the Son, the Creed expresses the community's belief that the Holy Spirit is divine. Indeed, the doctrine of the Trinity, according to Jaroslav Pelikan, is really "a doctrine about why Father, Son, and Holy Spirit must (as the Nicene Creed required) "be worshiped and glorified together."[11]

The doctrine of the Trinity was formulated out of the necessity to hold together belief in one God (i.e., monotheism) with the affirmation that God is Father, Son, and Holy Spirit. This doctrine preserves the divinity of the Father, Son, and Holy Spirit without falling into tritheism (i.e., belief in three gods) by maintaining that the one God exists as three persons. The Creed does not explicitly state formulaically that the one God exists as three persons. This formula is found in the summary statement of the Council.[12] Nevertheless, the Creed in its narrative form preserves monotheism by

---

10. J.N.D. Kelly, *Early Christian Creeds*, 2nd ed. (London: Longmans, 1960), 298. I have added the text in brackets for clarification and the italics for emphasis.

11. Jaroslav Pelikan, *Christianity and Classical Culture: The Metamorphosis of Natural Theology in the Christian Encounter with Hellenism*, Gifford Lectures at Aberdeen, 1992–1993 (New Haven & London: Yale University Press, 1993), 234. Here when Pelikan's refers to the Nicene Creed, he is really referring to the Nicene-Constantinopolitan Creed.

12. It is important to note that a copy of the council doctrinal decisions has not survived. The summary of the council's decisions comes from the "synodical letter of the synod of Constantinople held in 382, which expounded these doctrinal decisions, as the fathers witness, in summary form." Norman P. Tanner, S.J., ed., *Decrees of the Ecumenical Councils*, vol. 1, *Nicaea I to Lateran V* (London and Washington: Sheed & Ward and Georgetown University Press, 1990), 21.

affirming, in its opening lines, belief in *one* God ("We believe in one God") and then proceeding to explain that this God is Father, Son, and Holy Spirit. At the center of Christian belief and life is the doctrine of the Trinity, and as we have seen, the prayers of the community entered into its formation. Prayer informs doctrine; indeed, it figures in the formation of the central doctrine of the faith.

While prayer informs doctrine, doctrine also informs prayer. Let us reflect the doctrine of the Trinity back on our life of prayer to allow it to illuminate the fundamental belief operative in authentic Christian prayer. This underlying belief is that God has chosen to communicate himself, not a word *about* himself, but his very being and life. This is to say that "God himself, as the abiding and holy mystery…is not only the God of infinite distance, but also wants to be the God of absolute closeness in a true self-communication."[13]

Indeed, if we read Paul[14] in light of the doctrine of the Trinity, we can say that through the sending of the Son and the Spirit we are invited to enter into the inner life of the Trinity. It is through the activity of the Holy Spirit that we become like the Son, and as such, we become adopted sons and daughters of the Father so that we, like Jesus, can call the Father "Abba." The term *Abba* is a Greek transcription of the Aramaic abbā´, which means "father," but it is a term of intimacy that in Aramaic comes closer to meaning "Daddy" or "Papa." What is crucial here is not that we focus on the term "*father* as it connotes maleness, for the term *father* is a metaphor and God is neither male nor female. What is crucial is that we focus on the term *father* as an expression of intimacy. It is this intimacy with the Father that we are called to through the Son and Spirit. More precisely, it is through the activity of the Holy Spirit that we become like the Son and participate in the Son's intimate relationship with

---

13. Karl Rahner, *Foundations of Christian Faith*, trans. William V. Dych (New York: Crossroad, 1989), 137.

14. See Romans 8:15 and Galatians 4:6.

the Father. As such, we are invited to call God "Abba" or "Father" as Jesus did and we can pray as Jesus instructed us to pray, that is, we can pray the "Our Father."[15]

In conclusion, let us bring this understanding of Christian prayer to bear on our contemporary situation in which people refer to themselves as "spiritual, but not religious." While the different forms of meditation and practices for quieting and recollecting ourselves are helpful and although we, as a community, use both impersonal and personal language in our prayer, ultimately Christian prayer is to a God who is personal. The God of Jesus Christ is not only the ground of existence or some cosmic energy or the one who simply sets the universe in motion; rather, the Father of Jesus Christ has sent his Son and Spirit into the world so that we can draw close to him and share in his life, like the Son shares in his life in order that we "may have life, and have it abundantly."[16] This, I suggest to you, is the core of Christian faith and the heart of Christian prayer in all its diversity.

---

15. See the classic work, Joachim Jeremias, *The Prayers of Jesus*, trans. John Bowden, Dr. Christoph Burchard, John Reumann (Philadelphia: Fortress Press, 1967). See also Joseph A. Fitzmyer "Abba and Jesus' Relation to God," *À cause de l'Évangile: Études sur les Synoptiques et les Actes offertes au P. Jacques Dupont, O.S.B. à l'occasion de son 70e anniversaire*, Lectio Divina 123, ed. R. Gantoy (Paris: Cerf, 1985), 15–38.

16. John 10:10.

1. Prayer in the Old Testament

"How long, O, LORD?"—Lament in Prayer

Dianne Bergant, C.S.A., Catholic Theological Union

On September 14, 2001, I was invited to celebrate with a religious community on the occasion of its primary feast day, the Exaltation of the Holy Cross. The entire nation was still in shock because of the events that had transpired in New York, Washington, DC, and a Pennsylvanian field only three days earlier. The celebrant for the Eucharist was a major church leader. I sat dumbstruck, listening to a theological sermon on the meaning of the cross, while not a single reference was made to the catastrophe that had befallen us. Though at the appropriate time in the liturgy we did pray for the victims and their surviving families, our national grief was never really addressed, nor were we given an opportunity to mourn within the context of prayer.

In December 2004, I was in India, invited to lecture to a group of religious leaders. I had been in the north of the country on the twenty-sixth when the tsunami swept across the Indian Ocean, destroying everything in its path. The country was understandably traumatized by this tragedy: bewildered people not knowing where to go, what to do, or whom to contact. Several individuals who had registered for the conference at which I was to speak canceled, rightly believing that their place was with their people. While the scope of this natural disaster was still unfolding before our eyes, the celebrant of the Eucharist pointedly interpreted the catastrophe that was enveloping thousands of people as the just retribution of an avenging God. Once again, at the appropriate time in the liturgy we prayed for the souls of the victims, but no opportunity was given to us as a group to grieve as a group the loss of so many.

When the destructive floodwaters of Hurricane Katrina hit the Gulf Coast of the United States, we watched in horror as terrified people clung to rooftops, begging for help. We followed those who had been herded into civic buildings unequipped to meet their needs as they cried in anger and frustration for assistance that had been promised them.

In each one of these tragedies, we witnessed a remarkable surge of human compassion and an outpouring of hospitality and assistance. Heaven itself was deluged with prayer for those so sorely afflicted. But how much attention was given to the profound grief that took hold of so many, a grief that probably broke an untold number of spirits and soured countless more?

There seems to be so little room for grief in our prayer. How did such a stoic form of spirituality ever develop? And what a dispassionate image of God does it reflect? Even funerals often move quickly over understandable sorrow in order to rejoice in the life of the deceased. In many instances, we are told not to cry but to trust in God. The only kind of sorrow that is encouraged is sorrow for sin, which might actually be more a sense of guilt than of grief. This could well stem from our general perception of suffering as punishment for sinfulness. Under such circumstances, we may think that grief is inappropriate and we have no right to complain. However, we are not always responsible for our grief. Where did we learn that it is inappropriate to complain to God? This is not at all the frame of mind that we find in the Old Testament.

The ancient Israelites had no problem crying out to God in grief. We find laments in various places throughout the Old Testament. The form of speech that cries out against any type of suffering or loss, whether personal or public, is found in a funeral dirge in the First Book of Samuel, in prophetic mourning in Jeremiah, in the personal pathos of Job, and in psalms of lament. An examination of examples of these forms of speech provides us with insight into a little observed dimension of Israel's prayer and, perhaps, it will open us to the advantages of incorporating such sentiments into our own prayer.

"How the mighty have fallen" (2 Samuel 1:19)

The dirge or funerary lament, a public expression of grief, is considered a feminine genre because the professional mourners were women. However, the Second Book of Samuel contains two dirges sung by King David. The first appears on the occasion of the deaths of Saul and Jonathan, Saul's son and David's close friend (see 2 Samuel 17–27) and the second at the death of Abner, a commander in the army of Saul (see 2 Samuel 3:33–34). The following comments flow from a look at the first dirge.

[17] David intoned this lamentation over Saul and his son, Jonathan.
[18] (He ordered that The Song of the Bow be taught to the people of Judah; it is written in the Book of Jashar.) He said:

[19] "Your glory, O Israel, lies slain upon your high places!
How the mighty have fallen!
[20] Tell it not in Gath,
proclaim it not in the streets of Ashkelon;
or the daughters of the Philistines will rejoice,
the daughters of the uncircumcised will exult.

[21] You mountains of Gilboa,
let there be no dew or rain upon you,
nor bounteous fields!
For there the shield of the mighty was defiled,
the shield of Saul, anointed with oil no more.

[22] From the blood of the slain,
from the fat of the mighty,
the bow of Jonathan did not turn back,
the sword of Saul return empty.

> [23] *Saul and Jonathan, beloved and lovely!*
> *In life and in death they were not divided;*
> *they were swifter than eagles,*
> *they were stronger than lions.*
>
> [24] *O daughters of Israel, weep over Saul,*
> *who clothed you with crimson, in luxury,*
> *who put ornaments of gold on your apparel.*
>
> [25] *How the mighty have fallen*
> *in the midst of the battle!*
>
> [26] *Jonathan lies slain upon your high places.*
> *I am distressed for you, my brother Jonathan;*
> *greatly beloved were you to me;*
> *your love to me was wonderful,*
> *passing the love of women.*
>
> [27] *How the mighty have fallen,*
> *and the weapons of war perished!*
>
> 2 Samuel 1:17–27

This passage is explicitly identified as a dirge or *qinah* (verse 17). It received its name, *qinah*, from a particular type of rhythm suited for mourning. This is a kind of poetry wherein the lines lack balance. The first part of the line tapers off into a shorter second part, creating a plaintive lilt, almost a gasp. The dirge is introduced by the characteristic expression "ah, how," in Hebrew *'êkāh*, a word that also resembles a gasp. This same expression is repeated twice in the passage, almost as a refrain (verses 19, 25, 27). The dirge itself seems to have been a modification of a standard form known as "The Song of the Bow" found in an ancient collection of poems entitled *The Book of Jashar.*

The funeral dirge probably originated with the death of an individual, but it was soon used to mourn the demise of tribes, cities, and whole peoples. Its characteristics include the following elements: an opening cry of desolation; a summons to mourn; a declaration that death has occurred, accompanied by eulogizing the deceased; a description of reversal of fortune; an expression of the mourner's grief; a reference to the effect that this death is having on others; and an expression of bewilderment at what has happened. Several of these characteristics can be found in this passage:

- Opening cry of desolation—*"Ah! How the mighty have fallen"*
- Summons to mourn—*"He [David] ordered that The Song of the Bow be taught to the people of Judah"*
- Declaration of death and a eulogy—*"Your glory, O Israel, lies slain upon your high places...they were swifter than eagles, they were stronger than lions"*
- Description of reversal of fortune (a curse)—*"You mountains of Gilboa, let there be no dew or rain upon you, nor bounteous fields!"*
- Expression of grief—*"O daughters of Israel, weep over Saul...I am distressed for you, my brother Jonathan; greatly beloved were you to me."*

There is no explicit reference here as to the effect these deaths will have on others, nor is there an expression of bewilderment. However, most of the characteristics of a dirge are present.

The first part of the dirge, a call for public mourning, decries the death of both Saul and Jonathan (verses 19–23). After their military exploits are exalted, the daughters of Israel are summoned to mourn the death of Saul. This is probably a reference to a group of women who were professional mourners. However, their response to Saul's death is placed in stark contrast to the joyful reaction to his death on the part of the daughters of the Philistines (verse 20).

The dirge ends with an expression of grief at the death of Jonathan. This death was more than a public tragedy for David; it was also a personal loss of the one he loved like a brother.

There is no mention of God in this dirge. Perhaps the reason for this can be found in the origin of the genre. Funerary laments were often part of the ancient cult of the dead. Israel might have stripped this pagan practice of its religious character, leaving it as a very human expression of loss. However, in keeping with Israel's own theology, this song of grief contains no reference to punishment for sin, no anger directed toward heaven. It simply allows David the opportunity to give free rein to his anguish without any recrimination or vindictiveness. That is not to say that David lacked faith in God. Rather, it underscores our biblical ancestors' acceptance of the very real need to mourn. The text indicates that the dirge was "to be taught to the people of Judah," and was, therefore, not meant to be a religious poem but a heroic elegy. Although the biblical text itself may possess no explicit religious dimension, every aspect of ancient Israel's life was attuned to the divine. If this included success and failure in war, it would certainly encompass all those who were struck down fighting for Israel's cause.

"You duped me, O LORD" (Jeremiah 20:7, *NAB*)

The prophet Jeremiah lived during one of the most troubled periods that ever faced the kingdom of Judah. Besides its own internal troubles, that kingdom was caught in the middle of the conflict between Egypt and Babylon. The Egyptian ruler had proceeded to the Euphrates in Babylon. He was unsuccessful in this particular campaign and lost to the Babylonians a few years later. However, the tides soon turned and Egypt eventually defeated Babylon. This seesawing of political power was frequently played out on the corridor of the Fertile Crescent where the land of Israel is situated, resulting in a pull within the country between pro-Egyptian and pro-Babylonian loyalties. It was during a period of Babylonian ascendancy that Judah finally fell to Babylonian forces. This was the world in which Jeremiah lived.

Jeremiah was a reluctant prophet. He resisted his call to ministry, proclaiming: "Ah, Lord GOD! Truly I do not know how to speak, for I am only a boy" (Jeremiah 1:6); to which God replied: "Do not be afraid of them, for I am with you to deliver you" (verse 8). This reassurance on God's part might explain the prophet's eventual acceptance of his destiny. It also explains his pathos-filled complaint to God:

> [7]*You duped me, O LORD, and I let myself be duped;*
> *you were too strong for me, and you triumphed.*
> *All the day I am an object of laughter;*
> *everyone mocks me,*
> [8]*Whenever I speak, I must cry out,*
> *violence and outrage is my message;*
> *The word of the LORD has brought me*
> *derision and reproach all the day.*
> [9]*I say to myself, I will not mention him,*
> *I will speak in his name no more.*
> *But then it becomes like burning fire in my heart,*
> *imprisoned in my bones;*
> *I grow weary holding it in,*
> *I cannot endure it.*
> [10]*Yes, I hear the whisperings of many:*
> *"Terror on every side!*
> *Denounce! Let us denounce him!"*
> *All those who were my friends*
> *are on the watch for any misstep of mine.*
> *"Perhaps he will be trapped; then we can prevail,*
> *and take our vengeance on him."*
> [11]*But the LORD is with me, like a mighty champion;*
> *my persecutors will stumble, they will not triumph.*

In their future they will be put to utter shame,
    to lasting, unforgettable confusion.
[12]*O LORD of hosts, you who test the just,*
    who probe mind and heart,
Let me witness the vengeance you take on them,
    for to you I have entrusted my cause.
[13]*Sing to the LORD,*
    praise the LORD,
For he has rescued the life of the poor
    from the power of the wicked.

                        Jeremiah 20:7–13 (*NAB*)

This passage belongs to a longer section that is considered the final complaint of Jeremiah (20:7–18). The entire unit falls into two parts: the lament itself (verses 7–13) and a self-curse, brought on by the prophet's inability to endure suffering any longer (verses 14–18). The characteristics of a standard lament include an invocation of God's name; the complaint; prayer for help; reason for the need of help; a vow to offer sacrifice when the prayer has been heard; grateful praise of God. These characteristics can be identified here:

- Invocation—*O Lord*
- The complaint—*You duped me*
- Prayer for help—*Let me witness the vengeance you take on them* [his enemies]
- Reason for the need of help—*You were too strong for me, and you triumphed*
- Grateful praise—*Sing to the Lord, praise the Lord*

The verses under consideration here are basically all complaint, and it is all directed toward God. The poignancy is striking. Although the short passage does contain a description of what the prophet suffered at the hands of others ("derision and reproach all the day"), the primary focus is on God. It was God who called Jeremiah to the role of prophet and assured him of divine protection; it was God who allowed Jeremiah's enemies to prevail against him; therefore, God was responsible for his anguish. True, from the beginning, God had warned him that there would be suffering: "They will fight against you;" but there was also a promise of victory: "but [they] will not prevail over you, for I am with you to deliver you, says the LORD" (1:19). Jeremiah had borne the affliction, but where was the deliverance?

The suffering that Jeremiah's trusting in God caused him does not appear to have been torture enough, for the power of God that afflicted him was also irresistible. Jeremiah knew that calling the people to repentance would probably be to no avail. Nonetheless, he could not prevent himself from proclaiming God's word even more. There was no resolution for his dilemma. If he spoke God's word against Jerusalem, the city that he loved passionately, he would most likely engender hostility; if he did not speak that word, it would burn within him until he could bear it no longer. All he could do was turn to God in reproach.

This lament is unique in the Bible. Jeremiah is not accusing God of persecuting him, of inflicting misfortune of some kind; that was Job's complaint. Nor does he accuse God of abandoning him, as the psalmist cries out. Rather, Jeremiah accuses God of deceiving him, of overpowering him, and then leaving him defenseless. The Hebrew word for *duped* means "to seduce" and is used at times to refer to the seduction of a virgin. This accusation is almost blasphemous. Jeremiah is here claiming that God took advantage of his naiveté. The prophet admits that he allowed himself to be so seduced, but God had promised to be with him. Surely this meant that he would be successful as a prophet.

It was with religious passion that Jeremiah cried out *against* God, not merely *to* God. His reproach reflects a deep commitment existing between himself and God, one that the prophet felt had been violated by God, not by him. This complaint is the prayer of a man who, because of the sufferings that he was made to endure, decided to turn away from his appointed destiny, but could not. If the word of God burned within his heart and was imprisoned within his bones, it was only because Jeremiah had been open to that word in the first place. The reproach that he flung at God in no way altered that openness.

"I will complain in the bitterness of my soul" (Job 7:11)

In the popular mind, Job is remembered as a patient man. Afflicted by God, though he was innocent of transgression, he clung to his faith in God and in the end was rewarded for his fidelity.

Such a perception of Job is really a misperception. In the forty-two chapters of the book that bears his name, Job is patient in the first two chapters and in the last ten verses of chapter forty-two. In all the rest of the book, Job is a man who struggles with God's apparent injustice toward him and lack of concern over his plight. The real Job is not one who sits with bowed head in submission, but one who shakes his fist at heaven, demanding an explanation.

Throughout his dialogues with the men who came to visit him (perhaps they should be called monologues, because the speakers seem to be talking past each other), Job insists that he is innocent of any failing that might have occasioned the scope and depth of his afflictions. He argues that God has been unfair, has allowed some hardships to befall him, and has explicitly inflicted others. He also directs his accusations to God:

> My own utterance I will not restrain;
>   I will speak in the anguish of my spirit;
>   I will complain in the bitterness of my soul.
> Am I the sea, or a monster of the deep,
>   that you set a watch over me?

Why have you set me up as an object of attack?
 or why should I be a target for you?
When I say, "My bed shall comfort me,
 my couch shall ease my complaint,"
Then you affright me with dreams
 and with visions terrify me,
So that I should prefer choking
 and death rather than my pains.
I waste away: I cannot live forever;
 let me alone, for my days are but a breath.
What is a man, that you make much of him,
 or pay him any heed?
You observe him with each new day
 and try him at every moment!
How long will it be before you look away from me,
 and let me alone long enough to swallow my spittle?
Though I have sinned, what can I do to you,
 O watcher of [humankind]?
Why do you not pardon my offense,
 or take away my guilt?
For soon I shall lie in the dust;
 and should you seek me I shall then be gone.

Job 7:11–21 (NAB)

Job's first form of prayer in the dialogues is a complaint. It is not a technical lament as we found in Jeremiah. The Hebrew word means "meditation" or "musing." This complaint springs from inner reflection, from anguish of spirit and bitterness of soul. Job complains that he is being treated like God's mortal enemies, the sea or the monster of the deep. The references are to the mythological forces of evil that God fought and conquered in the primeval cosmic battle that preceded creation. Job cannot understand why God is treating him in this way, for he has been loyal in his commitment to God. God seems to have turned against him, betrayed him, and for no reason. He has become a target of God's attacks, and he is helpless before the power of his divine adversary.

Job realizes that there is nowhere to hide from God. His only recourse is sleep. There, momentarily away from the miseries of his life, he might be able to marshal his strength in order to face again the onslaughts of God's wrath. But not even there can he find respite, for his nightmares terrify him and he is victimized by visions. There is no escape, except, perhaps, in death.

In words reminiscent of Psalm 8, Job asks: "What is a man, that you make much of him?" (Job 7:17, *NAB*). The Hebrew word for *man* is 'ĕnôsh, a word that denotes a "weak, limited human being." There is no moral aspect here, only creaturely limitation. In the psalm, the question is meant to underscore the extraordinary dignity bestowed on a limited creature at the time of creation; in Job the same question highlights the incomprehensible difference between Job and his divine contender. This poor human creature is constantly under the watchful eye of the preying God. In his agony, he does not even have an opportunity to swallow his spittle.

There is a reference to retribution in Job's last words. He admits that he has sinned. However, he maintains that his punishment, if that is how he is to understand his misfortune, far exceeds the crime. He does ask for pardon, but he states that it would be to God's advantage to pardon him, for if he died, he would be out of God's reach for either added affliction or for any homage that Job might offer God. (The author of Job seems to have believed that the land of the dead was beyond the reach of the God of the living.)

In no way should we conclude that Job has turned away from God and is blaspheming. On the contrary, he believes that God has turned away from him. Job's visitors may have been appalled by Job's condemnation of God, but God does not seem to have been. In fact, at the end of the book God reprimands the three men who considered it their responsibility to defend God: "I am angry with you and with your two friends; for you have not spoken rightly concerning me, as has my servant Job" (Job 42:7–8, *NAB*). The men who chastised Job for his bold words are reproved by God, while the man who with stinging words reproached God is commended.

"Be gracious to me, O LORD, for I am in distress" (Psalm 31:9)

The average person is acquainted only with those passages from the Old Testament that are included in the liturgy as either lectionary readings or responsorial psalms. Even there, the selected verses usually serve to highlight some theme found in the New Testament, seldom the meaning of the Old Testament reading or psalm itself. Because Christian liturgy is primarily considered a celebration, the complaining verses of the laments are generally included only for funerals or during Holy Week. This is unfortunate, for there is much to be said for all the religious sentiments found in the laments.

Scholars believe that there were originally three parts to the lament. It began with an expression of complaint, which was followed by sentiments of confidence that God could and would remedy the misfortunate situation. The psalm then concluded with words of grateful praise. The progression of these sentiments is significant. As stated earlier, it is vital that anguished people be given an opportunity to express their grief. Their complaint to God should not be seen as a lack of faith. On the contrary, directing their grievance to God is an acknowledgment that God is indeed in control of the world and all that is within it. Such an acknowledgment is really an act of faith. Those who suffer are not in error when they complain; rather, they are in error if they do not move from that complaint to an expression of trust.

Trust in God may be one of the most difficult—because it is so often misunderstood—religious sentiments to nurture and sustain. Many people believe that it means that we trust that God will remedy the situation as we understand it, rather than trust that it will be remedied as God understands it, even though such a resolution may not be what we had hoped. At the end of his conflict, Job genuinely trusted in God, but not the way he had previously trusted. Before his experience of God emerging from out of the storm, he thought that God should explain why he, Job, had been afflicted in the first place. After his encounter with God, he no longer demanded answers. Instead he admitted:

> *I have dealt with great things that I do not understand;*
> > *things too wonderful for me, which I cannot know.*
> *I had heard of you by word of mouth,*
> > *but now my eye has seen you.*
> *Therefore, I disown what I have said,*
> > *and repent in dust and ashes.*
> > > Job 42:3-6 (*NAB*)

These words indicate that Job believed that all things were in God's hands, and he now trusted that God would provide as God saw fit. This is the kind of trust of which the psalm speaks. Only with this kind of trust, a trust that might appear to be blind, will we be able to move to the third and final expression of religious sentiment, that of grateful praise.

Psalm 31 is an example of a lament that clearly contains all three religious sentiments: complaint, trust, and gratitude. Throughout the poem we find evidence of lament. For example,

> *My life is worn out by sorrow,*
> > *my years by sighing.*
> *My strength fails in affliction;*
> > *my bones are consumed* (verse 11, *NAB*).

> *I hear the whispers of the crowd;*
> > *terrors are all around me.*
> *They conspire against me;*
> > *they plot to take me life* (verse 14, *NAB*).

These cries are followed immediately by sentiments of confidence:

> *But I trust in you, LORD;*
>> *I say, "You are my God."*
> *My times are in your hands (verses 15–16, NAB).*

The psalm ends on a note of gratitude and praise:

> *Blessed be the LORD,*
>> *who has shown me wondrous love,*
>> *and been for me a city most secure (verse 22, NAB).*

This ending presumes that either the prayer for deliverance has been answered, or the afflicted person has absolute confidence that it will be answered in the future. This psalm exemplifies the kind of trust seen in the book of Job. The psalmist declares: "Into your hands I commend my spirit" (verse 6, NAB); "I trust in you, LORD" (verse 15, NAB); "My times are in your hands" (verse 16, NAB). (It was not by accident that the Gospel writer placed the words of this psalm into the mouth of the dying Jesus: "Father, into your hands I commend my spirit" [Luke 23:46]. In fact, the psalm itself became a kind of commentary on the suffering of Jesus.) There is no mention of culpability or punishment in this psalm, only relentless affliction of various kinds. The issue here is not innocence or guilt; the issue is unrestrained lamentation in the face of acute suffering.

Though this psalm is clearly the prayer of an individual, there is an explicit communal dimension to it. Whether or not the setting of this psalm is cultic, as some scholars maintain, in the last verses, the suffering person turns to a congregation. This is not simply a random group of people. The Hebrew word describing them comes from the same root as *hesed*, the word for "covenant love." These are the faithful ones, the holy ones, the covenanted people of God. It is to them that the exhortation is directed:

> *Love the* LORD, *all you faithful,*
>   *The* LORD *protects the loyal,*
>   *but repays the arrogant in full.*
> *Be strong and take heart,*
>   *all you who hope in the* LORD.
>   Psalm 31:24–25 (*NAB*)

The community is called to witness the devotion of the psalmist, devotion that is expressed through words of complaint, trust, and gratitude. The psalmist is not calling attention to the suffering, unlike the poet of Lamentations who cried out:

> *Come, all you who pass by the way,*
>   *look and see*
> *Whether there is any suffering like my suffering,*
>   *which has been dealt me*
>   *When the* LORD *afflicted me*
>   *on the day of God's blazing wrath.*
>   Lamentations 1:12

Instead, the congregation is called to trust in God, as the psalmist has. These are words of encouragement: "Be strong and take heart / all you who hope in the LORD" (Psalm 31:25, *NAB*) They suggest that the psalmist is not the only one who is suffering.

These final words add a fourth dimension to this lament. What began in complaint, moved to trust, and ended in gratitude, now becomes a model for others caught in similar conflict situations. This is true not only for the members of the psalmist's congregation, but for those who, down through the ages, have endured misfortune of any kind and in their grief have turned to psalms of lament for understanding and encouragement.

"How long, O LORD?"

So often we hear that people turn away from the horrors of the world in which we live, because they are too terrifying and too multiple for them to comprehend or remedy. From the scenes of human carnage at Auschwitz to the fields of starvation in Darfur, from natural destructions in Indonesia to the fierce storms on the other side of the world, there is more suffering than can even be imagined. And what can we do? Even when we muster our resources and rush to the assistance of those who have been stricken, we can attend only to their physical needs. There seems to be little that we can do for their terror, their grief, their frustration, and their anger. Because most people have not experienced what the victims of such tragedies have experienced, they often seem to be unable to enter into the real agony.

And so we pray. We pray that those afflicted will be relieved of their suffering; we pray that they will be granted the strength they need to endure; we pray that they and we will be preserved from future catastrophe. But how often do we bring our grief to prayer? How often do we raise our voices and cry out, "How long, O LORD? Will you forget me forever? How long will you hide your face from me?" (Psalm 13:1). How often do we follow the lead of our ancestors in the faith and turn to God in lament, then to move to deep and genuine trust, and finally rest in grateful praise? If we do not engage in such a journey of faith, we will have lost an opportunity of profound religious experience. Furthermore, it is possible that we might flounder in our grief and turn away from God in despair. As always, the words of Jesus provide us with an example of prayer: "My God, my God, why have you forsaken me?" (Matthew 27:46; Mark 15:34); "Into your hands I commend my spirit" (Luke 23:46).

2. Prayer in the New Testament

Susan A. Calef, Ph.D., Creighton University

According to the Gospel of Luke, Jesus' disciples approached him with the request, "Lord, teach us to pray" (11:1). In the Letter to the Romans, Paul apparently knew what those first disciples knew, namely, "we do not know how to pray as we ought" (Romans 8:26). The words of these earliest followers of Jesus afford perhaps the most fundamental lesson the New Testament has to offer regarding prayer: prayer is something to be learned; perhaps more to the point, any disciple of Jesus needs to learn how to pray. Prayer does not come naturally, nor is it easy; indeed, because "we do not know how to pray as we ought," Paul informs the Roman community, "the Spirit helps us in our weakness" interceding "with sighs too deep for words" (Romans 8:26).

As modern-day disciples of Jesus, those of us gathered for this lecture series, one in spirit with our ancestors, request, as they did, "Lord, teach us to pray." The Second Vatican Council affirmed that sacred Scripture is "the very soul of sacred theology" (On Divine Revelation, *Dei Verbum* VI:24) and the pure and perennial source of the spiritual life (*Dei verbum* VI:21), and so, prayer in the Old and New Testaments is, rightly, our starting point. Much of what the New Testament teaches about prayer is in continuity with Old Testament traditions. Indeed, we find on the lips of Jesus laments found in the Psalter of ancient Israel. Having been enlightened by Dr. Bergant about this Old Testament prayer tradition, we turn now to ask, what might we learn about prayer from the New Testament?

A comprehensive survey of prayer in the New Testament would include Jesus' own practice of and teachings about prayer, to which the four gospels testify, as well as prayers, instructions, and comments about prayer found in the Acts of the Apostles, the Pauline and non-Pauline epistles, Hebrews, and the Book of Revelation. That amounts to a considerable body of material, to which we can hardly do justice given time constraints. Fortunately, several excellent surveys of prayer in the New Testament are readily available.[1] Alternatively, a narrower focus on how Jesus responds to the request that he teach the disciples to pray would permit a more in-depth look at the Lord's Prayer (Luke 11:2–4 or Matthew 6:9–13) and the instruction about prayer that accompanies it (Luke 11:5-13 or Matt. 6:5–8). Such an approach could well profit us; for, a prayer as familiar as the Lord's Prayer is for Christians is in danger of becoming mere words, recited thoughtlessly, without the attention requisite for true prayer. Choice of such a narrow focus, however, seems ill-advised, since detailed treatments of the Lord's Prayer, each affording fresh appreciation of the profound wisdom of this short and simple prayer, are also available.[2]

Therefore, to strike a balance between the breadth that surveys afford and the depth that choice of a single passage or two would permit, we will focus on Jesus as Teacher and Model of Prayer, and more precisely, Jesus as Teacher and Model of Prayer in the Gospel of Mark.[3] My reasons for that choice are several. First, that we are

---

1. Most notably, Robert J. Karris, *Prayer and the New Testament. Jesus and His Communities at Worship* (New York: Crossroad Publishing, 2000); also Richard N. Longenecker, *Into God's Presence. Prayer in the New Testament* (Grand Rapids, MI and Cambridge: Eerdmans, 2001).

2. Michael Crosby, *The Prayer That Jesus Taught Us* (Maryknoll, NY: Orbis, 2002); also N.T. Wright, *The Lord and His Prayer* (Grand Rapids, MI: Eerdmans, 1997); and Albert Haase, *Swimming in the Sun: Discovering the Lord's Prayer With Francis of Assisi and Thomas Merton* (Cincinnati: Saint Anthony Messenger Press and Franciscan, 1993).

3. In this chapter I use the term "the Markan Jesus" to signal that I am referring to Jesus as he is depicted in the Gospel of Mark and not as he is variously reconstructed by historical Jesus researchers. Because what can be learned from the New Testament regarding prayer is not limited to the words and deeds judged "historical" or "authentic" by historical Jesus researchers, I do not engage their conclusions and arguments for the purposes of this chapter. It is worth noting, however, that most of the sayings about prayer in the gospels are among those judged "authentic."

currently reading Mark in the lectionary cycle affords us a *kairos*, an "opportune time," for attending to lessons about prayer that can be learned from the Markan Jesus. Second, Mark, as the earliest Gospel, is widely assumed to have been used as a source by Matthew and Luke. Therefore, examination of prayer in Mark serves as a useful introduction to many, not all but many, of the teachings found in these later and lengthier Gospels. Third, the Gospel of Mark has been little appreciated throughout much of Christian history. Augustine's rather damning assessment—that Mark was but a digester of Matthew—appears to have had lasting impact, as Mark has suffered by comparison and still does today. This shortest of the canonical Gospels is, however, far more than a *Reader's Digest* version of Matthew. Intensive study of Mark in recent years has afforded me a deep appreciation for the spiritual resources that this earliest Gospel holds, among which I count Jesus' prayers in crisis, that is, his anguished prayers in Gethsemane (14:32–39) and on the cross (15:34).

Prayer in the Gospels

The essence of biblical prayer is conversation with God, the covenant partner. This does not mean, however, that the New Testament presents a narrow understanding of prayer as always requiring words. A careful analysis of the New Testament yields an understanding of prayer as at times wordless. Paul's affirmation that the Spirit prays in us "with sighs too deep for words" (Romans 8:26) suggests such prayer, as does Jesus praying through an entire night (see Luke 6:12), which surely was not continuous speech, but rather, silent presence and attention to God as well. Likewise, John's Gospel suggests there was an asking and receiving taking place between Jesus and the Father that did not always need to come to verbal expression. In John, which for centuries has been known as the "spiritual," even the "mystical" gospel, prayer is a sustained spiritual communion with and silent abiding in God.[4] Still, most biblical prayer, as conversation with God, involves addressing God in words, and that is generally the case for the Jesus we encounter in the Gospels.

All four canonical Gospels are consistent in portraying Jesus as a man of prayer who conversed with God and also on occasion advised others how to pray. The prayer life of Jews included prayers in the synagogue, grace before meals, and personal prayers in the morning, afternoon, and evening.[5] The evidence of the Gospels suggests that Jesus was no exception to this pattern (e.g., frequenting the synagogue, engaging in ritual prayer at meals, making festal pilgrimages to the temple in Jerusalem).

Not surprisingly, it is the Gospel of John, with its pronounced emphasis on the oneness of Father and Son, and so, on the divinity of Christ, which contains the most distinctive material about prayer. Jesus' public ministry in the fourth gospel features only two brief prayers of Jesus (see John 11:41–42; 12:28), and there is no instruction about prayer given to the disciples during the public ministry. All of the teaching about prayer is reserved for Jesus' farewell discourse (see John 13:1–17), where we also find his lengthy final prayer, known since the seventeenth century as the high-priestly prayer of Christ (see John 17:1–26). In it we hear the voice of the risen Christ praying for future believers, among whom we may count ourselves (see 17:20–21).

The treatment of prayer in Matthew is, arguably, the least distinctive, as its content is drawn largely from Mark and a second source (Q) also used by Luke. Matthew uses most of the material on

---

4. At the beginning of the third century, Clement of Alexandria referred to John as the "spiritual gospel." On mysticism and John, see also Sandra Schneiders, *Written That You May Believe* (New York: Crossroad, 1999); Demetrius R. Dumm, *A Mystical Portrait of Jesus. New Perspectives on John's Gospel* (Collegeville, MN: Liturgical Press, 2001); L. William Countryman, *The Mystical Way in the Fourth Gospel.* 2nd ed. (Valley Forge, PA: Trinity Press International, 1994).

5. For an introduction to Jewish prayers from the time of Jesus, see Karris, *Prayer and the New Testament*, 33–39.

prayer found in Mark, abbreviating it in some cases, and in others adding references to prayer in order to explain what is unclear or simply implied in Mark.[6] Also, in his handling of this source material, Matthew develops prayer into a topic in its own right within the Sermon on the Mount (see Matthew 6:5–15).

That prayer is especially prominent in Luke is widely acknowledged, hence, its designation by some as "the Gospel of Prayer." Luke opens with the jubilant prayers of Zechariah, Mary, Elizabeth, the angels, and Simeon in the infancy narrative (Luke 1, 2) and closes with the disciples in the temple praising God (Luke 24:52–53).[7] Statistically, Luke has far more material on prayer than Mark, Matthew, or John, including nine prayers of Jesus and three "parables" about prayer not found in any other Gospel (Luke 11:5–8; 18:1–8; 18:9–14).[8] Luke portrays Jesus praying at important moments of his life, for example, at his baptism (3:21) and before his choice of the Twelve (6:12). Similarly, in the Lukan sequel, Acts of the Apostles, the Christian community and its leaders are repeatedly shown at prayer.[9]

The Gospel of Mark, as previously mentioned, suffers by comparison to the later gospels, including with respect to the topic of prayer. Because Mark has less material about prayer than Luke, some conclude Mark has little to offer on the subject. Granted, the

---

6. For example, Matthew 19:13 clarifies what Mark 10:13 means by "that he might touch them," also, Matthew 26:42 specifies the content of Jesus' second prayer in Gethsemane so that his increasing resolve to do the Father's will is highlighted. Although the Matthean treatment of prayer offers little that is distinctive, worship receives much greater attention than in Mark; see Mark Allan Powell, *God With Us. A Pastoral Theology of Matthew's Gospel* (Minneapolis: Fortress, 1995), 28–61.

7. Luke's infancy narrative has given the Church three hymnic prayers: the Magnificat (1:46–55), the Benedictus (1:68–79), and the Nunc Dimittis (2:29–32).

8. See John Navone, *Themes of St. Luke* (Rome: Gregorian University Press, 1970), 118–131.

9. The first community is praying together in Jerusalem at the beginning of Acts (1:14) and, like Jesus, prays before choosing Judas' replacement (1:24–25). For the community at prayer, see also Acts 2:42 and 4:31. Individual disciples are also depicted at prayer, for example, Paul and Silas (16:25) and Peter and John (3:1).

amount of material on prayer in Mark is not extensive. The Markan Jesus speaks of prayer, in each case briefly, only six times (9:29; 11:17; 11:22–25; 12:40; 13:18; 14:38) and is depicted at prayer only seven times (1:35; 6:41; 6:46; 8:6–7; 14:22–23; 14:32–42; 15:34), far less indeed than in Luke. Such statistical comparisons are misleading, however, for the meaning and significance of prayer in Mark, or in any of the gospels for that matter, is not a function of mere quantity of references. As we will see, prayer features prominently in the dramatic climax of Mark's telling of the Jesus story. That Jesus' final and only words on the cross are in Mark, a prayer speaks for the theological significance of prayer for Mark and his community.

The Markan Jesus as Teacher and Model of Prayer

Turning now to the texts on prayer in Mark, I will focus our attention on those depicting Jesus at prayer, and more specifically, on the four texts in which his prayer is the focus of the episode.[10] My comments present an understanding of the meaning of each of these episodes based on the narrative logic of Mark's distinctive telling of the Jesus story.

Jesus, the "Christ" and "Son of God" (1:1), makes his initial appearance on the Markan stage as a man of the Spirit. This occurs immediately in the prologue (1:1–13), which consists of three brief scenes, each consisting of references to the Spirit (1:8, 10, 13), the crucial scene being Jesus' baptism in the Spirit (1:9–11). From that point on, Jesus lives in response to the promptings of the empowering Spirit of God that enters him at the baptism. On the first day of public ministry, he drives out an unclean spirit in the synagogue, leaving witnesses marveling at his incomparable authority (see Mark 1:21–28), heals Simon's mother-in-law (see 1:29–31), and by close

---

10. Three additional passages include the prayer gestures of thanksgiving or blessing (see 6:41; 8:6; 14:22–23), but because the focus of these episodes (see 6:35-44; 8:1-9; 14:17–26) is feeding, not prayer, they are omitted here.

of day, with people in need streaming to him, heals and exorcises many more (see 1:32–34).

On the next day, "In the morning, while it was still very dark, he got up and went out to a deserted place, and there he prayed" (Mark 1:35). References to the early hour and the deserted place suggest that Jesus was determined to slip away to a solitary place, so that he could be alone. Mark provides no information regarding the content of his prayer.[11] The point apparently is not *what* Jesus prays but that *he prays,* and that he does so immediately upon commencing his ministry. A similar reference later in the narrative confirms his rhythm of prayer and activity. After feeding the 5,000 (see 6:35–44), dismissing the crowd, and sending the disciples on another boat trip (6:45), Jesus "went up on the mountain to pray" (6:46). Once again Jesus makes a very deliberate withdrawal to a solitary place, this time in late day. By means of these references to Jesus' prayer at beginning (1:35) and well into his ministry (6:46), Mark suggests that private prayer forms the undercurrent of Jesus' life and ministry.[12]

The question for disciples like us becomes, then, is private prayer the undercurrent of our lives and work? From the example of the Markan Jesus we learn of the need to pray alone, by withdrawing from interactions with others. To do so requires a conscious effort to find time and space apart. According to Mark, Jesus' prayer times seem to have been early in the morning before the start of the day's

---

11. Elsewhere the Markan Jesus criticizes the scribes for saying long prayers as a public display or spectacle by which to win a reputation for piety (Mark 12:40). Other gospels clarify why prayers need not be lengthy, because "your Father knows what you need before you ask him" (Matthew 6:8). It is not surprising, then, that the Lord's Prayer (Luke 11:2–4; Matthew 6:9–13) is marked by an economy of words.

12. Although the text is silent on Jesus' motivation in each of these instances, the narrative logic of these chapters, which depict Jesus moving at a breathless pace, suggests that he did so because of a felt need to restore and center himself. In addition to feeling the need to withdraw to pray, Jesus also called his disciples away from the crowds in order to rest (6:31).

activities and interactions, and late in the day. Because he was an itinerant, the space for prayer depended on the circumstances at hand—on one occasion a deserted place, on another a mountain. For us, perhaps it is a quiet room in our homes, the far end of the backyard, or a nearby park or walking trail, in the car while waiting for children, or during the morning or evening commute.

Even if we have a space readily available, in the midst of our busy family and/or professional lives it is not easy to find the quiet, uninterrupted solitude for conversation with God. That is also the case for the Markan Jesus, as indicated by what transpires during his first withdrawal for prayer. Despite having slipped away early to a deserted location, while praying Jesus is interrupted, not by spouse, children, or neighbor, but by his disciples, who, in tracking him down, have their own ideas about what he should be doing. "When they found him, they said to him, 'Everyone is searching for you'" (1:36–37). These first recruits to his movement do not share or comprehend Jesus' need to pray before resuming his work on behalf of God's kingdom.

Jesus, however, is a man with a clear sense of purpose. In Mark, that purpose derives from the baptism, which is his adoption, anointing, and authorization as God's Christ and Son (1:9–11). As a result of that "in-Spiriting" baptismal experience, Jesus knows who he is, the beloved Son, and what he is to be about, doing the will of God who claimed him as Son. That prayer is the practice that keeps the Markan Jesus centered on the will of God, the source of his purpose, is confirmed later in Gethsemane, as we will see. Here and elsewhere in Mark, Jesus is not vulnerable to pressure from his recruits—"peer pressure" as we might call it. Others have their agendas for him, as do the disciples and those seeking him here. Jesus, however, knows what he is about, and what he is about (the reign of God; see 1:14–15) is ultimately for the good of them, but on God's terms. And so, he responds, "Let us go on to the neighboring towns, so that I may proclaim the message there also; for that is what I came out to do" (1:38). In narrative context Jesus' appealing, even enviable, centeredness is the fruit of his wise recognition of the need to pray.

The disciples, however, are eager to resume the previous day's activities. Their observation, "Everybody is looking for you," seems to suggest, "Let's pick up where we left off yesterday." Whether they are motivated by a genuine concern for the crowds of needy people looking for Jesus' help or are simply caught up in the excitement of his growing "celebrity," relishing glory by association like some sort of Jesus groupies, or a bit of both, is not clear. The text is silent on the matter of motivation. Nevertheless, the behavior of the disciples in this scene proves instructive regarding one of the temptations for discipleship in our time and culture, a compulsive "busyness," even if that "busyness" be about good things, including ministry.[13]

Jesus wisely resists such "busyholism" and whatever glories are attached to it, but the disciples are sorely tempted by it. Given their recent recruitment and the glorious start to Jesus' mission on day one, their conduct may be construed as the first fervor of novices. But, as we know, fervor fades or flounders, especially in times of trouble, without the rootedness that is sustained by a life of prayer. In Mark, Jesus is a man of action urgently on the move. His activity, however, is not compulsive but free, not aimless or willy-nilly but purposeful, the fruit of "life in the Spirit," which includes private prayer.

A further lesson about threats to discipleship in our lives emerges from this episode, namely, the ever-present temptation to forsake our discipleship for our own lordship. The disciples track Jesus down, seemingly with the intent of leading him back to the crowds seeking him. As the call of the disciples earlier in the narrative makes clear, however, discipleship is about walking behind Jesus, following his lead (see Mark 1:16–20). In the life of disciple-

---

13. Contemporary spiritual writers frequently remark that the proverbial "rat race" of life threatens to leave us with little time or energy for the prayer and reflection necessary for the centeredness that characterizes the life of the Markan Jesus.

ship, as in the life of Jesus, prayer is a lived acknowledgment that I am not in charge, not "Lord" of my life, or anyone else's. Rather, the disciple follows Jesus, who seeks ever to do the will of God; and doing the will of God, as the example of the Markan Jesus teaches, requires prayer.

This link between prayer and doing the will of God is modeled for disciples in the climactic events of the Gospel, above all in the Gethsemane episode, which features, for the first time in Mark, the content of Jesus' prayer, as well as a lesson about the need to pray in time of crisis. After celebrating the Passover meal with his disciples (see Mark 14:22–26), Jesus again withdraws to pray, this time with his disciples (14:32). Then, "He took with him Peter and James and John, and began to be distressed and agitated. And he said to them, 'I am deeply grieved, even to death; remain here, and keep awake.' And going a little farther, he threw himself on the ground and prayed that, if it were possible, the hour might pass from him" (14:33–35).

A startling change in Jesus' demeanor is dramatically evident here. Prior to this, Jesus spoke matter-of-factly, even with emotional detachment about his "destiny," three times declaring, "the Son of Man must suffer, die, and after three days rise" (8:31; 9:31; 10:33–34).[14] But in Gethsemane, with the "hour" now at hand, the

---

14. That the Markan Jesus is unflustered about this "destiny" is further indicated by 14:19, 27, and 30. In Mark's narrative logic, this remarkable attitude derives from his conviction that what he will undergo is willed by God. The first of his three passion predictions (8:31), with its use of Greek *dei* ("must" or "it is necessary"), indicates that this suffering, dying, and rising is the will of God. His statements in the Last Supper episode (14:21, 27), with their reference to "as it is written," also interpret his destiny as willed by God. In acknowledging that *dei* (8:31) implies the will of God, it is important to recognize that the three predictions all include reference to the resurrection; thus, they claim, not that God willed Jesus to suffer and die, but rather, that God willed him to suffer, die, *and* rise. According to the Markan narrative, God wills to reign, and so, raises up a Messiah and Son to march on Jerusalem proclaiming that reign. Everything that the Markan Jesus does on behalf of that reign, then, is an expression of the will of God: his preaching, healing, and exorcising, by which human suffering is relieved, as well as his own suffering, dying, and rising that will liberate from the power of death.

prospect of suffering and dying becomes for Jesus a grave crisis. The nature of that crisis is clarified by what is, in Mark's Gospel, Jesus' final instruction to his disciples: "Keep awake and pray that you may not come into the time of trial [in Greek *peirasmos*]; the spirit indeed is willing, but the flesh is weak" (14:38).

Because this instruction is occasioned by Jesus finding the disciples asleep, readers often assume that his comment targets the willing spirit and weak flesh of the disciples, who have so obviously embodied these realities.[15] But this pointed lesson for the disciples is based on what Jesus knows of his own spirit and flesh at this moment. Jesus experiences the arrival of the "hour" for the drinking of the "cup" as a *peirasmos,* which in Greek bears the threefold meaning of test, trial, and temptation; and he does so, by his own admission, because "the spirit is willing but the flesh is weak." In biblical thought the human person is flesh and spirit, but it is the flesh that is vulnerable to pain and death,[16] and so, vulnerable to temptation *(peirasmos)*, in this case, the temptation to flee in fear, which for Jesus would mean abandoning the "way of the Lord" (1:2–3) willed by the Father. Such temptation is simultaneously a test or trial, the other two meanings of *peirasmos,* for the prospect of pain and suffering that tempts one to flee in fear simultaneously serves to try and test one's fidelity to and trust in God and God's will. In Gethsemane, Jesus feels sorely tempted, tried, tested; and

---

15. The Markan disciples show themselves "willing in spirit": on the way to Jerusalem James and John declare their readiness to drink the cup that Jesus drinks (10:39); and after their Passover meal, to Jesus' prediction of his denial Peter responds with the vehement declaration, "Even though I should have to die with you, I will not deny you" (14:31), to which Mark adds "and they all spoke similarly" (14:31). That their flesh is weak, however, is amply evidenced in the events of the passion narrative: Peter, James, and John are unable to stay awake and pray with Jesus in Gethsemane (14:37, 40, 41); Judas betrays Jesus (14:43–45); all the disciples flee at his arrest (14:50); and Peter denies Jesus not once, but three times (14:66–72).

16. On the association of the flesh with weakness, see, for example, Genesis 6:3; Psalm 78:39; Job 34:14–15.

so, he admonishes the disciples to watch and to pray in order that they may not undergo a *peirasmos* as he does, in other words, that they may not find themselves in the position of having to flee or to deny him. The disciples, however, fail to heed the Master's counsel, as three times Jesus finds them not awake and praying but asleep. And so, later in the scene, their willing spirits falter under the weakness of the flesh as they flee, abandoning Jesus in order to save themselves (14:50).[17]

In stark contrast to the sleeping disciples, Jesus deals with the *peirasmos,* this crisis of the flesh, through prayer, which he knows to be powerful (9:29; 11:24) and which proves to be so here. The prayer begins with intimate address ("Abba, Father"), followed by an expression of faith, "all things are possible for you," that acknowledges the freedom and power of God to accomplish whatever God wills. Then, in the context of the relationship of trust implied by the intimate address, Jesus voices a stunningly forthright request: "...remove this cup [in other words, this measure of suffering] from me" (14:36). In his conversation with James and John on the way to Jerusalem, Jesus had spoken, without flinching, of "the cup that I drink" (10:38)[18]; and in the Passover meal that immediately preceded the withdrawal to Gethsemane, with no sign of distress Jesus had declared over the shared cup, "This is my blood of the covenant, which is poured out for many" (14:24). But now Jesus'

---

17. At the arrest in the Gethsemane episode, the disciples embody the typical response of "the flesh" to threat, that is, self-preservation by fight or flight: one resorts to the sword (14:47) and in the end, all flee (14:50). On the Markan stage the last appearance and the final words of any disciple belong to Peter, who was the most vehement about his willingness to die with Jesus (14:31). With the words "I do not know this man about whom you are talking" (14:71, *NAB*) for the third time Peter denies not self, as a disciple ought (8:34), but Jesus, in order to save his skin.

18. In biblical tradition, "cup" often symbolizes the fixed amount of whatever God has to offer a person. In the prophets and psalms, the image of emptying a cup is used for the suffering that must be endured; see Isaiah 51:17, 22; Jeremiah 25:15; 49:12; 51:7; Habakkuk 2:16; Psalm 11:6; 75:9.

willing spirit is tried, tested, and tempted as his flesh, vulnerable to pain and death, and so, to fear, recoils at prospect of actually drinking the cup. Significantly, the desire of Jesus' flesh is at odds with what he knows to be the will of God; but he does not hesitate to express that contrary desire to the Father. Then, in the midst of extreme distress, as if strengthened by prayer, Jesus manages to add, "… yet, not what I want, but what you want" (14:36). Lest we think the words "not what I will but what you will" end his struggle, note what follows. After getting up and finding the disciples asleep, "And again he went away and prayed, saying the same words" (14:39). Jesus persists in prayer, voicing his petition a second, and even seemingly, a third time (14:37, 39, 40), while the disciples fall to sleep.

Jesus' prayer-petition is not answered in Gethsemane, the heavenly voice that sounded at the baptism (1:11) and transfiguration (9:7) remaining mysteriously silent.[19] By the end of the scene, his spirit steadied, Jesus' crisis of the flesh has passed. Although a very human fear rooted in "the flesh" threatened to undermine his willing spirit, and so, his obedience, ultimately, Jesus' faith (i.e., his trust in and fidelity to the Father), did not falter.[20] Braced by the power

---

19. On what is typically referred to as the problem of "unanswered prayer," Paul's experience bears consideration. Apparently the apostle experienced a problem that he describes as a "thorn…in the flesh" and "a messenger of Satan" (2 Corinthians 12:7). The nature of the problem (a sickness or physical disability, a handicap impacting his apostolic work, an opponent, a temptation) continues to elude scholars. Paul reports that "Three times I begged the Lord about this, that it might leave me, but he said to me, 'My grace is sufficient for you, for power is made perfect in weakness'" (2 Corinthians 12:8–9). Like Jesus in Gethsemane, three times Paul petitioned God for deliverance from this affliction, but evidently, again like Jesus, his petition was not granted, as the "thorn" was not removed. His remarks indicate, however, that he believed his prayer was answered, albeit not in the way he had hoped. We do not and cannot know how and when this "answer" came to Paul, that is, when he recognized the divine response. The experience of Christians suggests that at times what we think initially to be prayer unanswered turns out to be prayer answered differently than we had hoped; also, often the answer is seen only in hindsight, which, unlike sight or foresight, is 20/20.

20. Mark's Gospel, with its critique of abusive authority and its God and Jesus story-line, affords valuable insights regarding the relationship of trust, obedience, and authority.

of prayer, Jesus resolves to drink the cup: "The hour has come; the Son of Man is betrayed into the hands of sinners. Get up, let us be going. See, my betrayer is at hand" (14:41–42). As will be evident on the cross, however, Jesus' steadfast resolve to entrust himself to Abba's will does not lessen the pain that his flesh soon undergoes nor does it exempt him from a terrible sense of forsakenness when plunged into the depths of the paschal mystery.

The Gethsemane episode affords several lessons for disciples seeking to learn how to pray. The most obvious is Jesus' instruction to his disciples: "Watch and pray that you may not undergo the test; the spirit is willing but the flesh is weak" (14:38). With this Jesus alerts disciples to the reality and workings of *peirasmos,* that is, situations that tempt, try, test our fidelity to Christ and the gospel. Due to the hazards they pose, we ought "watch and pray" in order that we not find or put ourselves in such situations.[21] Jesus' counsel reflects a wisdom about the flesh, with its very human instinct for self-preservation and avoidance of pain, suffering, and death, be it physical, financial, emotional, psychological.[22] Due to its vulnerability to pain, injury, and assault, the flesh, as the "Achilles heel" of our discipleship, can impede our ability to walk "the way of the Lord" behind Jesus[23]; and so, we need to be awake and to pray that we will not find ourselves in the trying situations that tempt us to flee or to compromise our commitment to the Gospel.

---

21. The counsel to pray in the face of *peirasmos* replicates a petition in the Lord's Prayer, "lead us not into *peirasmos,*" that is, into the test, trial, temptation (Luke 11:4; Matthew 6:13).

22. Under the influence of later dualistic thought, Christians often associate "the flesh" with sexuality, sin, and evil. This is not the biblical understanding, which reflects Hebraic thought according to which God created us flesh and spirit. Reflective of that view, Jesus does not claim that the flesh is evil, simply that it is weak, that is, vulnerable to those forces adverse to God's will to reign.

23. On my reading, the essence of the spiritual wisdom of Mark's Gospel is captured in Jesus' observation, "the spirit is willing, but the flesh is weak"; hence, the title of my current book project, *Willing Spirit, Weak Flesh: A Markan Spirituality of Discipleship.*

In addition to his explicit instruction to his disciples, the Markan Jesus models for us the courage to pray when experiencing *peirasmos*. Courage is required in order to pray because at such times fear, which in Mark is the antithesis of faith, can paralyze us, render us mute, tempt us to despair. Just as prayer restored the oneness of will that had characterized the Markan Jesus' spirit until the crisis in Gethsemane, so, too, fervent, persistent prayer has the power to render our spirits willing when our flesh is weak, when our very human desire to avoid the costliness of discipleship tempts us to forsake "the way of the Lord" upon which we walk behind Jesus.

Finally, from the Markan Jesus in Gethsemane we can learn much also about the attitudes proper to prayer, including and perhaps especially with respect to petitionary prayer. In this regard each element of the content of Jesus' prayer proves instructive. The address "Abba," suggestive of intimacy and trust like that between parent and child, presupposes a humble recognition of our dependence on and need for God. Such intimacy and trust, of course, is not a given for us; rather, as in any relationship, it is something to be developed and deepened over time, through shared life and communication, and so, through the practice of prayer such as that which marked Jesus' life.

The words "if it is possible" (14:35) imply our freedom to bring our requests to God, while also acknowledging God's freedom to reject or grant our petitions. God desires to hear anything and everything from us; but so, too, the pray-er must be open to hearing anything and everything from God, letting God be God in the covenant-conversation that is prayer. The related affirmation, "Everything is possible for you" is an expression of the confidence that is both source and product of all prayer; for the one who prays submits needs and desires to God precisely because he or she believes in God's power to accomplish whatever God wills.

The petition, "Take this cup away from me," suggests that we, like Jesus, ought to come to the conversation as we are, flesh and spirit, praying with an honesty that reflects profound trust—in this case, trust that frank speech is not inappropriate to conversation with God; moreover, that there is nothing, not even desires that we suspect are at odds with God's will, that ought be withheld in prayer. Indeed, from Jesus' example in Gethsemane we learn that prayer requires an openness that is twofold, openness about our own desires, needs, and hopes ("Take this cup away from me") and openness to the conversation-partner ("yet not what I will but what you will"). The depth of faith required to be able to pray with such openness is not a given for us; indeed, it represents for us an ideal from which we fall short at times. But such faith can be developed, as apparently it was for Jesus, by the ongoing conversation that is prayer.

Moreover, that Jesus, even after saying these words the first time, continues to plead for the cup to pass suggests that they did not instantly resolve the matter or make things easier for Jesus and that they will not do so for us. Jesus' own very human desire for self-preservation was not magically extinguished by their utterance; rather, the desire of his flesh persisted, and so, his struggle continued. But Jesus persisted in prayer, and through the power of that prayer, the desire of Jesus' flesh did not have the last word in Gethsemane. Rather, his willing spirit did: "not what I will but what you will." With these words Jesus denied the prompting of his own flesh, thereby denying himself (see Mark 8:34), because his spirit, that which attuned him to Abba, willed to do what the Father wills.

In summary, then, the Markan Jesus in Gethsemane teaches us that faith is the fundamental attitude required in prayer. Earlier Jesus had called for faith in prayer, enough to move mountains (see Mark 11:23–24), affirming, "whatever you ask for in prayer, believe that you will receive it, and it will be yours" (11:24). His own example in Gethsemane clarifies what that faith entails: confidence that God's power can move mountains ("all things are possible for you") and an openness that bespeaks deep trust in the good and loving will of Abba ("take this cup away from me; yet not what I will but what you will").

This brings us to the final prayer scene in Mark 15:34, which reads, "At three o'clock Jesus cried out with a loud voice, *"Eloi, Eloi, lema sabachthani?"* which means, "My God, my God, why have you forsaken me?" In Mark these are the only words of Jesus on the cross and they are his last words.[24] They are the hardest of the seven last words of Jesus to hear, confronting us as they do with the unspeakable pain of flesh and the deep anguish of soul that Jesus, in the fullness of his humanity, experienced on the cross.

Mark's crucifixion scene emphasizes that Jesus dies terribly alone. The disciples, those with whom he had shared bread and cup, are nowhere to be seen, the solidarity of road and table now painfully broken; and so, Jesus hangs on the cross in a kind of solitary confinement, with none but his executioners and enemies, ridiculing and taunting him, making sport of his powerlessness (see 15:29–32). Mark's tolling of the hours draws attention to a mounting anguish that reaches a crescendo with two agonized cries (see 15:34, 37): the first three hours marked by mockery and ridicule (15:25–32), the next three, by an invading darkness, which in the ninth hour, with Jesus' cry, appears to envelop, even penetrate him, swamping his soul.[25]

Remarkably, Jesus makes no complaint to taunting bystanders and executioners. But note that Jesus does not die quietly, docilely, submissively. Rather, he lifts his voice to the heavens: "My God, my

---

24. Also Matthew 27:46. Luke omits this cry, instead substituting words that echo Psalm 31:5 (Luke 23:46). The cry of dereliction is also not found in John.

25. This is "the baptism that I am baptized with" about which he spoke earlier (10:38). The Greek verb *baptizo* suggests plunging. Although we associate baptism with washing, in the Old Testament it meant the plunging and total submersion of a person in the terrifying depths of waters in which one could drown (see Psalms 42:7; 69:2–3; Isaiah 43:2; 2 Samuel 22:5). What the Markan Jesus must undergo as "Son of man," suffering, dying, and rising, is such a fearsome plunging.

God, why have you forsaken me?" (15:34). In this, Jesus does what the suffering righteous of his people had done for generations: he cries out to God, in this case, with the opening words of Psalm 22. In the many lament psalms, the people of Israel had, for centuries, brought to their covenant-God their experiences of negativity, of pain and distress, of injustice and innocent suffering. These laments are often referred to as the psalms of the suffering righteous. And the Markan Jesus is surely a suffering righteous one, one in right relation with God. His walk on "the way of the Lord" began with his baptism in the Spirit when the heavenly voice claimed him, "You are my Son, the beloved; with you I am well pleased" (Mark 1:11). Subsequently, this Son lived up to those words, proclaiming the in-breaking of God's reign among his people, healing the sick, freeing the possessed from the grip of evil, feeding hungry crowds, even embracing the "mystery" (4:11, *NAB*) that the coming of God's reign would require far more than glorious mighty deeds (8:31; 9:31; 10:33–34). In Gethsemane, this Son, experiencing that "the spirit is willing but the flesh weak," struggled mightily and prayerfully through his crisis of the flesh. Jesus, then, comes to the cross every bit the trusting obedient Son, God's righteous one, only to experience the atrocious absence of Abba.

And so, to die alone, bereft of the felt presence of the Father, this Son finds senseless. Indeed, in narrative context the absence of Abba threatens to strip Jesus of the one thing not yet taken from him: the conviction that this terrible happening is not as absurd as the taunts of bystanders suggest, that in truth it has meaning. The Son has come to the cross believing this to be the will of God[26]; and

---

26. The Markan interpretation of Jesus' fate is found on the lips of Jesus during the journey to Jerusalem—"The Son of Man is to be betrayed into human hands, and they will kill him, and three days after being killed, he will rise again" (8:31; 9:31; 10:33–34) and "The Son of Man came not to be served but to serve, and to give his life a ransom for many" (10:45)—and at the Last Supper—"This is my blood of the covenant, which is poured out for many" (14:24).

so, the question that now torments him, why Abba's absence? What does that absence mean? Might it imply God's disavowal of Jesus? The Markan Jesus' last words are, then, not a last-minute cry for divine intervention; in Gethsemane he had entrusted himself to Abba's will. They are, rather, a cry for God. They are a cry for that divine presence on which the meaning of this terrible event depends, a cry for meaning and for solidarity.

These last words are also a cry of protest, expressive of the anger of a beloved son who trusted in and obeyed, who counted on, and who now needs Abba to be with him, in the depths of mystery into which he is plunged. Although troubling to many Christians,[27] Jesus' conduct here is consistent with the faith and prayer practices of ancient Israel. For, the lament psalms in Israel's prayer book are bold speech, the kind of bold speech that occurs in the deep and durable committed relationship called covenant, that began with God's declaration of election, "I will take you as my people, and I will be your God" (Exodus 6:7; Leviticus 26:12). In the context of Israel's covenant-life with Yahweh, the lament psalms, including Psalm 22, are a complaint that insists: "Things are not right here! They can be changed. God, you make it right!"[28] Similarly, Jesus'

---

27. To many Christians, Jesus' cry on the cross sounds like a cry of despair that seems inappropriate, even inconceivable, on the lips of the Son of God. Therefore, to render it less theologically problematic, they claim that Mark intends us to recognize that Jesus prayed the entirety of Psalm 22, which concludes with praise and confidence in deliverance by God (Psalm 22:23–32). Such an interpretation softens the dereliction and protest with which these interpreters are uncomfortable, but at the expense of the Markan text and its narrative logic. The cry must be interpreted based on Mark's text, without importing meanings from other gospels (for example, Luke 23:46) or later Christian theology. In Mark, it is an unmitigated cry of dereliction; however, because it is addressed to God, it is not a cry of despair.

28. In his treatment of the lament psalms, Old Testament scholar Walter Brueggemann contends that "in both complaints concerning failed human hesed and unresponsive Yahweh, the issue is justice"; moreover, that by their regular use, Israel kept the justice questions alive and legitimate. See Walter Brueggemann, "The Costly Loss of Lament," *Journal for the Study of the Old Testament* 36 (1986): 57-71, esp. 63.

special relationship with God, his sonship, began with a declaration of election from the heavens, "You are my Son, the beloved; with you I am well pleased" (1:11). In the context of that divinely-initiated relationship, Jesus' lament is the beloved Son's bold cry of protest that this terrible aloneness is not right, not the way it should be. It is, as it was for his fellow Jews, speech that bespeaks a bold faith that dares to cry for justice to the heavens, source of all justice.[29]

On Golgotha, there is no reply to this protesting cry for presence and for meaning. As at Gethsemane, the heavenly voice remains deadly silent. At the denouement of the Markan drama, however, we learn that Abba did not, ultimately, abandon his Son, for there is the good news delivered by the young man at the tomb, "you are looking for Jesus of Nazareth, who was crucified. He has been raised" (16:6). God's unfathomable will—that the Son of Man "must" suffer, die, and rise—is accomplished. The Crucified One is raised up and once again on the way to Galilee where the disciples will see him (see 16:7). Thus, Jesus' undying and sorely tried trust in Abba is vindicated, and the will of Abba proves worthy of that trust.[30] For Mark and his community, that will is "the beginning of the good news of Jesus Christ, Son of God" (1:1).

What can disciples learn from the example of the Markan Jesus on the cross? Above all, Jesus' lament on the cross authorizes us to pray as he did, with bold speech; for, it affirms that ours is a God

---

29. Brueggemann contends that this form of prayer-speech attests to the courage and ego strength with which Israel came before Yahweh in prayer; furthermore, that these prayers testify that God wills to relate to "a responsible, mature covenant partner who can enter into serious communion and conversation. In such a serious conversation and communion, there comes genuine obedience, which is not a contrived need to please, but a genuine, yielding commitment" (Brueggemann, "Costly Loss," 61).

30. For the reader who follows the God and Jesus story line in Mark, Jesus' cry on the cross, the narrative and theological climax of Mark's Gospel, raises the question, can God be trusted? Within Mark's narrative logic, the resurrection may be construed as God's answer to Jesus' anguished prayers in Gethsemane and on the cross: to Jesus' "yet not my will but yours," in the resurrection Abba answers, "My will be done," and that will is, for Mark and his community, "Gospel," good news.

who does not expect us to be docile "yes women" and "yes men," praying prayers of praise and thanksgiving when in the depths of our souls we are anguished, isolated, feeling forsaken. To be an Easter people does not require feigned joy and gladness when life brings brokenness and the cross; rather, the Markan Jesus would have us take a lesson from our faith ancestors in ancient Israel whose prayer book included personal and communal laments. Like our Jewish forebears, we ought, as individuals and in the liturgical assembly, dare to raise our voices to the heavens in complaint and in protest when things are "not right" in our lives and in our world, including when things feel "not right" between us and the one to whom we, too, may cry "Abba" (Romans 8:15; Galatians 4:6).[31]

Christians, however, are not comfortable with lamentation and complaint; such speech striking us, variously, as whining, or impertinence, or a sign of lack of faith. The example of the Markan Jesus on the cross surely ought to disabuse us of such notions. Some simply consider lament unnecessary and inauthentic, since they themselves feel no need to protest or complain. Such a position, however, betrays a lack of understanding of liturgical prayer

---

31. Having noted a neglect of the lament form in our liturgical assemblies, biblical scholars and pastoral theologians are now calling for the recovery of this form of prayer. Their work suggests that praying the laments in the liturgical assembly is a necessary means of facing, with one another and with our God, "what is not right," that is, the justice concerns of our lives and world. Brueggemann clarifies what is at stake in their costly loss: "A community of faith which negates laments soon concludes that the hard issues of justice are improper questions to pose at the throne, because the throne seems to be only a place of praise.…If justice questions are improper at the throne (which is a conclusion drawn through liturgic use), they soon appear to be improper questions in public places, in schools, in hospitals, with the government, and eventually in the courts [to which I would add, in churches]. Justice questions disappear into civility and docility. The order of the day comes to seem absolute, beyond question, and we are left with only grim obedience and eventually despair" ("Costly Loss," 64). The laments are also a valuable but underused resource for Christian ministries of care, such as work with victims of sexual assault or domestic violence. See Sally Brown and Patrick D. Miller (eds.), *Lament. Reclaiming Practices in Pulpit, Pew, and Public Square* (Louisville, KY: Westminster/John Knox, 2005).

in Christian life. In discussing the liturgical use of the psalms, Old Testament scholar Carroll Stuhlmueller commented, "In the liturgy, each one of necessity prays the prayer of everyone else….The psalms pull a person out of…psychological introversion and thrust him into the Church at large. Americans need to be reminded that there are other people in other lands at the edge of despair; healthy people must remember there are those who are lonely, hungry and dying….The liturgy brings all persons together, so that what one person lacks the other person supplies 'for the building up of the body of Christ'" (see Ephesians 4:13).[32] In other words, in the liturgical assembly, even if I as an individual do not identify with the words of a particular psalm or prayer, I am called to pray it with the community and with the praying Christ on behalf of others. I would further suggest that the practice of lament in the liturgical assembly provides a much needed rhetoric of solidarity in these fragmented and highly individualistic times.

To conclude, the prayer of the dying Jesus authorizes our lamentation in the face of the unspeakable suffering and calamity, the grave injustices that people experience in our times. On 9/11, nearly three thousand innocent people died in New York, among them numerous courageous rescue workers. Might not our churches have given voice to what was in the souls of their loved ones and their fellow citizens? "My God, my God, why have you forsaken us?" The twentieth and now twenty-first centuries have been ravaged by genocide. Those who saw *Hotel Rwanda* perhaps recall the scene in which, with the massacre coming, the white tourists at the hotel are quickly loaded onto buses to escape the violence that will soon erupt. Paul, the hotel manager, and his fellow Rwandans, however,

---

32. Carroll Stuhlmueller, *Thirsting for the Lord. Essays in Biblical Spirituality* (Garden City, NY: Image Books, 1979), 125–26. Similarly, Dietrich Bonhoeffer wrote, "Even if a verse or a psalm is not my own prayer, it is nevertheless the prayer of another member of the community" (Dietrich Bonhoeffer, *Life Together, in Dietrich Bonhoeffer Works*, Vol. 5 [Minneapolis: Fortress, 1996], 55).

are not permitted to board the buses to make an escape with the others. It is for me one of the most heart-wrenching scenes in all of film: with the whites looking out the bus windows at Paul and those he has been sheltering at the hotel, standing together in the rain, the buses drive off, abandoning these people to the coming slaughter. At a time such as that, should we not pray in solidarity, "My God, my God, why have you forsaken me?" Might such a prayer uttered in faith move mountains of indifference and mobilize peoples, churches, and governments to action? In a still more recent time and closer to home, recall the countless images of Hurricane Katrina victims, most of them poor and black, waiting for rescue, on rooftops, in attics, in hospital and nursing home beds. They waited on Monday, on Tuesday, on Wednesday, and were still waiting on Thursday and on Friday for a deliverance that, for many, did not come in time. Watching those painful, shameful images on the news, did we not hear the voice of the Crucified One, crying in solidarity with Katrina's victims, "My God, my God, why have you forsaken us," calling us to solidarity?

Indeed, when the darkness is so deep that we can see no help forthcoming, from heaven or from earth, the Markan Jesus would have us know: it is not right! And so, it is time to lament, to cry out of the depths and into the darkness for the Presence that still matters. Yes, disciples like us have much yet to learn in order to pray as Christ did. "Lord, teach us to pray" as we ought, alone and together, often and boldly.

3. *Lectio Divina:* The Meditative Reading and Praying of Scripture

Very Reverend Gregory Polan, O.S.B., Abbot of Conception Abbey

Thus far today you have heard about Biblical prayer, which is at the heart of our Judaeo-Christian faith. The prayer of Jews in the Old Testament was sacred for Jesus and his followers, who were Jews. It not only gave them words to address to God, but it also taught them how to pray, what to pray for, and to see that there is nothing in our human experience which cannot be lifted up to God and be understood as sacred. From gratitude to lament and everything in between, we find it all in the Scriptures. From the poetry of the Psalms to the Christological hymns of the New Testament, there is indeed a vast category of prayer to God. Yet even wider, broader, and more vast is the whole of Scripture when seen as a source for prayer, as a springboard to prayer. That is what we would like to do now—to see how God's word, the whole of Scripture, offers us a way to listen and to respond to our God who speaks to us through biblical passage after passage, from Genesis 1 to Revelation 22.

There are two major segments to this presentation. First, we want to see what is essential to using the word of God as a source of prayer. In our mind, what do we think of when we want to use the word of God as an avenue to our own prayer? And second, we want to look at an age-old and time-tested approach to using the Scriptures as a source of prayer, called in its Latin title, *Lectio Divina*, or Sacred Reading, or Prayed Reading. It is a reading of Scripture that has prayer as its goal, prayer which flows out of the word of Scripture and is closely connected to our human experience and the movements of our hearts as people of faith.

To illustrate the first segment of this presentation, let's listen to a story, a selection from *The Tales of the Rabbis*, which can be divided into three sections, each giving us a progressive sense of how one approaches the word of God as a source of prayer.[1] Section I we will call "Study."

I. Study

There once was a young boy named Mordechai. His parents loved him dearly. He was the perfect child, except for one thing. He refused to study the Word of God. It did not matter to him that all the boys his age were studying Torah. He would not do it. His parents promised to give him anything he wanted. They threatened him with everything he didn't want, if only he would study Torah. But come what may, young Mordechai would not study the Word of God.

His parents were at their wits' end. They did not know what to do. Then, one day, they heard that the Great Rabbi was coming to visit their village. They were delighted. "Surely he will be able to get Mordechai to read Torah," they said to one another.

When the Great Rabbi arrived, the parents took young Mordechai to him. "Our Son is a fine boy," they explained, "except for one thing. He refuses to study the Word of God."

"You give this boy to me," the Rabbi shouted, "and I will teach him a lesson he will never forget!" The parents were frightened by the Rabbi's rage. "Should we give Mordechai to this angry bear of a man?" they asked themselves. "Yet what else can we do?" So they handed young Mordechai over to the Rabbi.

---

1. The whole of this rabbinic story is found in Francis Dorff, *The Art of Passing Over: An Invitation to the Art of Living Creatively* (Mahweh, NJ: Paulist Press, 1988), 22–23.

In the last forty-plus years, we have been blessed to live in a time when a vast array of opportunities have been made available for us to learn more about the Scriptures. I am old enough to remember that as a boy, the Bible occupied a place on a coffee table in our living room. Yet in those days, the family Bible did two things: it kept family sacramental records and it collected dust. It was rarely read because it was understood as being beyond our understanding; in our Catholic grade school we learned Bible stories, and that was all. Today, our Bibles contain the kind of user-friendly introductions that help us understand the sacred texts found in them; they give us insight into biblical history, language, culture, and interpretation. Top-notch scholars are writing books that are inspiring and enriching reading for the nontechnical reader. Books like Bible dictionaries, commentaries, and dictionaries of biblical theology open up a universe of meaning to help us understand the word of God in wonderful ways that can truly touch our lives. While it can be fascinating reading, more importantly, it awakens us to the richness of the word of God which holds the potential to nourish our faith, our thirsting spirits. As we learned from Dianne Bergant, it makes a difference to know that a lament expresses a movement of faith, from expressing pain and struggle, to then voicing confidence and hope in God's saving action, and ending with praise and thanks to the God who brings redemption into our lives. That is the kind of study that speaks to the heart of faith, and shows us the rich expression of trust which underlies the literary form of a lament. Examples could abound, but suffice it to say that study is essential for praying from the word of God in an informed manner. As Christians living in the spirit of the Second Vatican Council, it is essential that we take time to study and understand the biblical texts, not as scholars but as informed and faith-filled readers.

II. Listening

The Rabbi grabbed Mordecai, led him into the next room, and slammed the door behind them. Young Mordechai stood in the corner of the room trembling. The Rabbi just stood there looking at him. "Mordechai," he whispered, "come here."

The young boy inched his way over to the Great Rabbi who stood with arms wide open. Without saying a word, the Rabbi folded his arms around the young boy and held him silently, against his heart.

After a while, the Rabbi took young Mordechai by the hand and led him to the door. Then, all of a sudden, he flung open the door and threw the young boy into the room where his parents were waiting. "I have taught the boy a lesson he will never forget!" the Rabbi shouted. "You mark my words. From this day forward he will come to know Torah."

This second section of the rabbinic tale is probably the most captivating, and yet the most mysterious. What is at play here in relation to the Word of God? The message is about the importance of listening in a unique way. The listening is described as something that comes from the inside, from the heart. And here we might borrow that expression that comes to us from the opening Prologue of *The Rule of Saint Benedict*, listening with the ears of our heart. There are some implications that come from this expression that are worth our consideration. When we listen with our heart, we listen with a rare openness. How much of our day is filled with various voices that bring us complaints, concerns, requests, or questions? And understandably, with so many words, we listen often half-heartedly at the many voices that barrage us and compete for our attention each day. And what are the practical implications of this on prayer?

All too often when we come to prayer, the first thing we do is begin talking, speaking, interiorly verbalizing. Yet when we pray from the Scriptures, the very opposite is true. We begin by listening to the word of God, to hear what God has to say to us first. And if we have listened to that word, then our word becomes a response, a true prayer, an answer to what God has initiated with us.

There are significant transformations that come from this approach to prayer through the Scriptures. When God's Spirit-filled word finds a welcome within our spirit-filled heart, a mysterious and wondrous movement of grace takes place: Spirit speaks to spirit. Within us there is a profound resonance that takes place; we are drawn to listen ever more deeply because of the new life that is engendered in us. We listen differently; we see life and people differently; we find ourselves acting differently—prompted by the word of God, which has led us to pray. When we listen from the heart to what God speaks to us, we find ourselves listening to others in the movement of our day in a different way—might I say, a way that leads to a new kind of openness, realizing how God wishes to speak to us in the divine word, but also through one another. When we come to the liturgy, we listen with a new awareness and depth. Our heart moves into prayer so naturally, responding to what God speaks to us through the sacred word. Like Mordechai, we've learned what it means to listen with our heart.

III. Know the Power of the Word

And so it was. Young Mordechai studied the Word of God as no one in the village had ever studied it before. He learned it all by heart. His parents were so proud of him.

As the years went by, Mordechai himself became a great Rabbi. People would come to him with their problems. They would marvel at the breadth of his wisdom and the depth of his compassion. In their amazement, they would often ask, "Rabbi, who taught you to read the Torah?"

Mordechai would smile and say, "I first learned to read Torah when the Great Rabbi held me and taught me to listen from my heart…to listen…from my heart."

This final section of the rabbinic tale demonstrates the power of the word of God to transform and change our lives. The word possesses a power to transform us into "a living word of God"; the word of God is incarnated by us. As the story goes, Mordecai learned to take the word of God to heart by reading it from the inside out. By "reading it from the inside out," we mean discovering the heartbeat of the message, the life blood that pulsates through the body of the scriptures. When we come to that point in our reading of the Scriptures, we are drawn to prayer, a response to the God who communicates with us through his word. Our reading from the Scriptures is something that is oriented toward both prayer and life. When our prayer flows from the reading of the word of God, a formative process is taking place within us. We are in the process of being formed anew by the word. As the text of Genesis 1 reminds us, the word of God is a creative power: God speaks a word and creation comes into being—"God said, 'Let there be light' (1:3); and there was light" (1:7). For us also, the word of God can become a creative force in our lives, directing our actions, our speech, our attitudes, our relationships, and our work with one another. As the story about Mordecai reads, "The people would marvel at the breadth of his wisdom and the depth of his compassion." The word of God schooled him in divine wisdom and formed him by holy compassion, which he in turn generously offered to others. Here is where we see the sacramentality of the word of God: when the proclaimed word becomes a living word. When the community and its individuals become so identified with the word of God that they are transformed by its power, they become the living word of God in our midst. The community and its individual members become a sacrament of the word of God—a sign pointing to the reality of

God's word in our midst, a sign distinguishing the power of God's word in our world.

With that background, let's talk about *Lectio Divina*, a sacred manner of reading the word of God accompanied with personal prayer. We should begin by noting that the practice of *Lectio Divina*, Sacred Reading, or Prayed Reading, often associated with monastic or Benedictine spirituality, began considerably earlier than Saint Benedict. We hear of spiritual leaders in the early centuries of the Church like Origen, Saint Ambrose, Saint Jerome, Saint Augustine, Saint Gregory the Great, all of these theological giants give us hints about what *prayed reading* is all about. For centuries, this practice of reading the Scriptures, reflecting on them, and praying from them came to be the daily spiritual diet of Benedictines, and eventually those orders associated with *The Rule of Saint Benedict.* However, it is important to note that, as a structured and articulated way of reading and praying from the texts of the Bible, the practice of *Lectio Divina* does not take its present form and shape until the twelfth century. It was the prior of the monastery of the Grand Chartreuse in France, Guigo II (d. 1188), who wrote the systematic fourfold approach of what we call *Lectio* (reading), *Meditatio* (meditation or reflection), *Oratio* (prayer), and *Contemplatio* (contemplation). What we would like to do in this second major segment of this presentation is to talk about what each of these four rungs on the spiritual ladder to *prayed reading* means.

Lectio (Reading)

When we sit down to read a newspaper, magazine, sports page, or novel, we come with an attitude, a mindset about how this is to be read. We usually read a magazine with less intensity and at a quicker pace than we do something from a textbook, an academic writing, or even a letter from a personal friend. The question before us is,

"How do we read a text of Scripture when, in the end, we want to be able to pray from it?" First of all, there is a certain preparation necessary: a calming of the heart, a quieting of the mind, a genuine sense of what we are about to do. The reading of this biblical text will be the voice of God speaking to me, and it will carry a message that needs to be given care and attention. The haste and quick pace of reading the newspaper is the exact opposite of the way that the Scriptures should be read in doing *prayed reading*. In his work, *Prayer as Meditation* (*Orationes sive Meditationes*), Saint Ambrose writes, "When we read the words of Scripture it should not be in agitation, but in calm; not hurriedly, but slowly, a few [words] at a time, pausing in attentive reflection [...] Then the reader will experience the ability to kindle the ardor of prayer."[2] Not unlike prayer, the reading of Scripture should not be hurried, but done deliberately, so as to see each word, even the conjunctions, prepositions, and the articles, as influential to our understanding of what God may speak of in this sacred text. It is the kind of reading which is done, and this is said without exaggeration, "one word at a time." The reading of the text is done over and over again. Saint Augustine used a vivid image to describe this kind of reading. He said it is like "a cow chewing on her cud." The grass in her mouth is chewed over and over again, so as to be digested easily. We can think of Ezekiel eating the scroll that is given him, so that it becomes a part of him.[3] The prophet is told, "Mortal, all my words that I shall speak to you receive in your heart and hear with your ears" (Ezekiel 3:10). The same is true for us in reading the Scriptures. We might consider another expression from our own day, "reading as to memorize," or "reading as to put to heart" the text before us. That is how one reads when doing *Lectio Divina*.

---

2. This quote is found in Mariano Magrassi, *Praying the Bible: An Introduction to* Lectio Divina (Collegeville, MN: Liturgical Press, 1998) 105–06.

3. See Ezekiel 2–3:11.

Meditatio (**Meditation, Reflection**)

In talking about meditation on the word of God, there are two wonderful sources that give us insight into understanding this; one in the twelfth century and the other in the twentieth: Guigo II, the Carthusian, and the Jewish philosopher and theologian Abraham Joshua Heschel. First, Guigo II wrote, "When meditation busily applies itself to this work, it does not remain on the outside, is not detained by unimportant things, but climbs higher, goes to the heart of the matter, examines each point thoroughly."[4] This is further explained by quoting Heschel who wrote, "To meditate is to know how to stand still and to dwell upon a word." To dwell upon a word in silence is to enter into the human heart to recall how the experiences of life have touched us in such a way as to leave us reflecting on what this means to my faith, my relationship with God, my relationships with family, friends, coworkers, neighbors, and even the nature that surrounds me. The language of the Scriptures draws us into some of the most elemental, yet most important values, beliefs, longings, and hopes of the human heart. For a moment, let us look at Psalm 25.

> [1]*To you, O LORD, I lift up my soul.*
> [2]*O my God, in you I trust;*
> *do not let me be put to shame;*
> *do not let my enemies exult over me.*
> [3]*Do not let those who wait for you be put to shame;*
> *let them be ashamed who are wantonly treacherous.*
>
> [4]*Make me to know your ways, O LORD;*
> *teach me your paths.*
> [5]*Lead me in your truth, and teach me,*
> *for you are the God of my salvation;*
> *for you I wait all day long.*

4. Magrassi, *Praying the Bible,* 108–09.

Be mindful of your mercy, O LORD,
and of your steadfast love,
for they have been from of old.
Do not remember the sins of
my youth or my transgressions;
according to your steadfast love remember me,
for your goodness' sake, O LORD!

Good and upright is the LORD;
therefore he instructs sinners in the way.
He leads the humble in what is right,
and teaches the humble his way.
All the paths of the LORD
are steadfast love and faithfulness,
for those who keep his covenant and his decrees.

For your name's sake, O LORD,
pardon my guilt, for it is great.
Who are they that fear the LORD?
He will teach them the way that they should choose.

They will abide in prosperity,
and their children shall possess the land.
The friendship of the LORD is for those who fear him,
and he makes his covenant known to them.
My eyes are ever toward the LORD,
for he will pluck my feet out of the net.

Turn to me and be gracious to me,
for I am lonely and afflicted.
Relieve the troubles of my heart,
and bring me out of my distress.
Consider my affliction and my trouble,
and forgive all my sins.

Consider how many are my foes,
and with what violent hatred they hate me.
O guard my life, and deliver me;
do not let me be put to shame, for I take refuge in you.
May integrity and uprightness preserve me,
for I wait for you.

Redeem Israel, O God,
out of all its troubles.

In just reading the first five verses, who of us here does not have life experiences which touch on trust, trust cherished and trust betrayed? Who of us here has not known the pain of waiting, waiting for God to answer our prayer, waiting for death to pay its final visit to a loved one, waiting for a loved one to return from a long trip away? Who of us has not struggled to *know* God's ways, has not desired to *understand* and *follow* God's ways, has not *looked* for God's ways in feeling lost? And what does it mean for God to teach us: *what* will God teach us, *how* will God teach us, *when* will God teach us the path to follow in life's sometimes perilous journey? That is the language of Scripture, and that is what it means to be still and to dwell upon a word. Our lives resonate with the word of God because God has used human instruments, people like you and me, with all their struggles and joys, their failures and successes, their pains and hopes, to relate to us the path of redemption and salvation. The great monastic founder and leader, Saint Bernard (d. 1153), would say to his monks that the "book of experience" and the Book of the Word resonate with one another; we find our own experience of salvation and redemption echoed in the pages of Scripture by reading them in such a manner as to reflect on the meaning of the words with calm and peace, with open heart and searching mind, with ready faith and with genuine charity. Thus we can readily recall with young Mordechai what it means to read from and meditate on the Scriptures from the heart, from a heart given over to listening with faith, to see life's meaning unfold with the power of God's word.

Oratio (Prayer)

Slow and repetitive reading, followed by open-hearted meditation and reflection, lead us to prayer, praying from the word of God. What we are now to talk about lies at the heart of *Lectio Divina, prayed reading*. In both our reading and in our meditation on the word, God speaks to us. Now in prayer, we respond to the voice and message of God. The heart that has been touched by reading and meditation now turns to prayer. Another way of saying this is that our prayer is the human response to the divine initiative, believing that God speaks to us through the Scriptures, revealing to us both the Lord of all creation and the unfolding plan of our redemption. For each and every one of us, we find our own salvation history in the pages of Scripture; our response to that plan of God comes forward in our prayer—how we see that plan unfolding, what our role in that plan is, how we have responded to it in the past, and how our deepest desires direct us into the future in following God.

One of the other distinct features of praying from the Scriptures is that it "teaches us how to pray." What do I mean by that? The Scriptures show us the ways of God, the truths of God's love, the challenge of living in accord with God's word, and the great dignity bestowed upon us as men and women, made in the image and likeness of God. To pray out of that knowledge and belief is a powerful avenue of prayer. While we may come to prayer with out list of needs and wants, if we enter into the texts of Scripture, read and meditate upon them, they will show us what to pray for. Often they will surprise us, because what "we think we need most," is far from what the word of God reveals to us about our greatest needs as children of God.

Again to return to Psalm 25 and to review those opening five verses, we can consider its message as an avenue for prayer. Look with me at that text. To say to God, "O my God, in you I trust," is a powerful acknowledgment of faith and confidence. But how often can we say we have trusted, surrendered our hopes, and placed ourselves before God, knowing what we hope for, yet trusting that God will lead us where we should be? Does our trust allow us to give God "a blank check" and wait to see what is written on it? To pray, "Make me to know your ways, O LORD, teach me your paths" is a powerfully risky expression of faith. All too often we know how the words of Isaiah resonate with our own experience, "For my thoughts are not your thoughts, nor are your ways my ways, says the LORD" (55:8). When we pray out of the Scriptures, there can sometimes be a brutal head-on confrontation with our own lack of fidelity, and our personal need for conversion. And there can be a tremendous comfort in knowing the truth of our own struggle, to realize the many generations of people who have recited and reflected on these same words, and continued to make them their own. And we know that such conversion lies at the heart of the paschal mystery, which is to follow Jesus. So we see that praying from the Scriptures is a powerful reality check, and I must add, a great consolation and comfort.

Contemplatio (**Contemplation**)

One need speak the least about contemplation, because what we do here is to rest in both the meditation and the prayer that have preceded. In contemplation, we remain in the presence of God with the word we have heard and the response we have made. In that sacred place, we abide with the word and allow it to sink its roots deep within us, becoming one with us, where mind, heart, body, soul, and spirit become one in the life-giving work of God's Spirit within us.

What we have considered today, I would normally take over an entire semester with our novices at the monastery. And in conclusion, I would simply state that the daily practice of *Lectio Divina* has been the most formative experience of my life as a monk, priest, and abbot. It is where I have heard the voice of God, which has enabled me to discover the voice of God in so many other places, often unexpected, but readily received. *Lectio Divina*, if we believe it to be the voice of God to us, forces us to listen and be attentive to the God who speaks to us all the time, in so many places, and desires of us a response, a response that is prayer, prayer of the heart, prayer of faith, and prayer of love.

4. The Liturgy: The Communal Prayer of the Catholic People

Mary Collins, OSB, The Catholic University of America

This conference on Prayer in the Catholic Tradition is giving us the opportunity to consider the core traditions of our faith and practice, to reaffirm them, and to reclaim the spiritual riches that are ours. It is my privilege to speak about liturgy, the most visible, the most public, and the most readily identifiable expression of Catholic praying. I am going to make three points. The first: liturgy is the communal prayer of the Catholic people. The second: Catholic liturgy is the way we pray together that gives expression to the core relationships that shape our Catholic identity. The third: just as the official Roman liturgy forms us as the people of God becoming the Body of Christ, so local communities at worship are always shaping the Church.

Liturgical Prayer Is Communal

The first point—that liturgy is the communal prayer of the Catholic people—was a major emphasis of the Second Vatican Council. But it was not a new idea. The communal character of liturgical prayer was clear everywhere in the first Christian millennium. In the second millennium, identifiable social and theological currents in the Western Church led to changed practices. Liturgy became privatized in a number of ways, with the focus on the ordained to the exclusion of the baptized. The communal nature of liturgy was never denied, but it faded from expression in conventional practice.

Theologians and Church historians in the nineteenth century began rereading the writings of Augustine and other Fathers of the Church. They also read accounts of the eucharistic practices of the Church in Jerusalem (Egeria) and also in the city of Rome, even as the imperial order was taking over. They found astoundingly clear records of a communal understanding of public worship. What they found laid the foundations for the principles stated clearly in *Sacrosanctum Concilium,* the Second Vatican Council's constitution on the sacred liturgy (1963). Liturgical praying requires the active and attentive participation of all the faithful. Yes, there are differences in liturgical ministries. But each liturgical role is essential. The poet e. e. cummings once called a parade "a big long line of everybody." Similarly, the Sunday eucharistic assembly is an intentional gathering of all the baptized.

Even newly baptized infants can and should be drawn into the actions of the liturgical community. A newly baptized toddler being held up for the community's acclamation during a parish Sunday Mass suddenly recognized that something big was going on, and he clapped with us and smiled back. During an Easter Vigil, four adolescent boys were charged with relighting seven red hanging sanctuary lamps during the parish's singing of the "Gloria." This was active and intentional participation, parish-style for teenage boys, during the Church's most solemn liturgical celebration of the year. Liturgy well celebrated can engage all the baptized, each according to their gifts and the ministries given.

Currently there is a magisterial and theological debate about whether the postconciliar emphasis on the liturgical assembly has resulted in an "idolatry" of the assembly. Some fear a dangerous overemphasis on the real presence of Christ in the assembly at the expense of acknowledging the priest as the one who ministers *in persona Christi.* Other voices express concern that an objectification of the real presence of Christ in the eucharistic species of bread has been the dangerous overemphasis, making the Eucharist a thing rather that a liturgical thanksgiving memorial. The conciliar document, in its famous paragraph 7, clearly affirmed that the real presence of Christ is to be found, not abstractly objectified, but alive by the power of the Holy Spirit: in the baptized assembly, in the scriptural word, in the ministering priest, and in the eucharistic species. The witness of the ancient and still living tradition to the mystery of our faith may elude our human sense of what is reasonable, leading us to think that it is up to us to choose our own focus. But the truth is that theologians and the magisterium alike are left to struggle with the intelligibility of the mystery.

Catholic Liturgy Is About Essential Relationships

Each of us is the person we are because of the relationships that confer our identity upon us. That is obvious in the matter of our families, whose names we wear. It is more subtle and more complex in the matter of our culture. What does it mean to be an American? No single opinion prevails. At the level of individual identity, personal preference becomes even more prominent. The clothes we wear, the foods we select, and the cars we drive tag us—wittingly or unwittingly—as participants in our consumer culture, just as surely as the wearing of gang symbols gives adolescents a dangerous and faulty but real sense of belonging. All these things function as displays of established identities, trial identifies, emerging identities. The young are particularly vulnerable to selecting identities. "Be all that you can be" is the slogan on the recruiting poster.

Yet at the level of core identity—who we are and what we are doing here—the stakes are great. As children some of us learned to recite answers to the questions "Who made me?" and "Why did God make me?" just as we learned our names, addresses, and phone numbers. But in a pluralistic culture, where routine changes in identity are possible and often attractive, it is easy for us to forget who we really are at the core, why we are here in the first place, and where we are going. Even those of us who still know our childhood catechism lines may recognize the truth in T.S. Eliot's lament, "we remembered the words but forgot the meaning."

The Catholic liturgical practice—even obligation—of gathering weekly, on Sunday, for the Eucharist, means to exercise us in the relationships we *must not* forget. We live in mystery, mystery disclosed to the world in the person of Jesus Christ. Artist Corita Kent once said the purpose of the liturgy was "remembering together who we are and saying 'yea,' ceremonially." *Remembering— together—ceremonially*—all are each operative words here. In our liturgical assemblies we open ourselves together to our core relationship with the Holy. We do this in order to affirm the relationship, to reconfirm it, and to deepen it. Let's explore this, if only briefly.

The Holy in whose embrace we are held is mystery. The mystery has been shown to us, we believe, in the person of Jesus Christ. The mystery is self-giving love. The God Jesus reveals to us is loving communion. In our Sunday eucharistic liturgy, we remember and celebrate that embrace.

Our eucharistic liturgy is Trinitarian because our faith is Trinitarian. There is audacity at the heart of Christian faith, audacity in our firm belief that the One God is Three Persons in communion. This Oneness in Three/Three-ness in One sets us apart from our Jewish and Muslim brothers and sisters. They share our belief that God is one, the God of Abraham, Isaac, Jacob, and the prophets. But they find incomprehensible, perhaps even idolatrous or blasphemous, our Trinitarian understanding of God and our conviction that Jesus Christ is God incarnate in human history. Our audacious Trinitarian belief sets us apart, too, from our Buddhist, Hindu, and animist brothers and sisters. The Buddhists give no credence to a saving God, believing that such faith is a diversion from dealing with the mystery of human suffering. Hindus and animists with whom we share life and our planet honor many gods to deal with their many human needs.

But we are Christians, men and women who have been given the gift of faith to believe that Jesus Christ is the Way, the Truth, and the Life. Jesus is the Way to life with God. Jesus is the Truth about life with God. Indeed Jesus is Life outpouring onto the Church and the world through the Holy Spirit, so that we humans might be transformed and live the mystery of loving communion as the world's salvation.

Our liturgy is redundantly Trinitarian in its symbols and ritual actions. We begin with a Trinitarian gesture, naming the Father, Son, and Holy Spirit, as we mark the cross on our own bodies, commonly with the holy water of our baptism. When we leave the eucharistic assembly, we are blessed and sent in this same way. During our liturgical action, we address our prayer to God, through Christ, by the power of and in union with the Holy Spirit. Our *Gloria* is a Trinitarian song of praise; our *creedal* statement of belief is Trinitarian.

The biblical texts we listen to show us facets of the Trinitarian mystery—now this moment, now that—all of it pointing us toward Jesus Christ and the outpouring of the Holy Spirit. The homilist shows us how to recognize the mystery within which we are already living. (British writer Rosemary Haughton once wrote astutely that the religious texts we learn by heart are the words of those already transformed—the apostles and prophets—and that they are given to us to prepare us for our own transformation, our entering deeply into the mystery of our lives in God.) Further, not only are our words Trinitarian, but our ministerial interactions are communal, an alternating of persons in communion offering and receiving holy gifts from one another in the course of doing our liturgy.

The great eucharistic prayer is our prayer of thanksgiving for the mystery. At its core is the narrative of the self-gift of Jesus. The mystery of Jesus Christ is this: he gave his life that the world might have life. In opening ourselves to the mystery of Christ week by week over a lifetime, we are taking the risk of having to die to ourselves. We are often resistant. Can we trust that we will really become our truest selves by giving ourselves, in order that others might have abundant life? Can we trust the God who trusts us and invites us to the table?

For a variety of historical reasons, the Trinitarian heart of the eucharistic mystery was not a dominant theme in our speaking or teaching about the eucharistic mystery. In our awareness, Jesus and God seemed the prominent actors. It was the work of nineteenth- and twentieth-century theologians like Yves Congar and Edward Kilmartin, who brought the Church once again to recognize the Holy Spirit in the foreground of every act of the people of God, most centrally, the Eucharist of the Church.

But artists can give expression to spiritual realities that elude speech. Many of us are familiar with Rublev's fourteenth-century Russian icon of the Trinity. Perhaps you know that, at the request of Pope John Paul II, it was one of four religious pictures inserted in full color in the original Vatican edition of the *Catechism of the Catholic Church*. Rublev writes what appears to be a biblical scene of the three visitors who come to Abraham and Sarah, the story told in Genesis. The three are seated around a table the couple set. Strangely, the icon bears the name "Trinity." Yes, there are three in communion. Each is distinct; yet they are One, each directed to an Other. As we look more closely, we see that the table has a single filled dish. Is it a chalice—holding drink? Is it a bowl—holding a meat dish? Commentators have named the vessel variously but have always recognized as eucharistic symbols the cup Jesus offered to his disciples with the question, "Can you drink of the cup of which I must drink?" or perhaps the slain Lamb victorious now found before the throne in the Book of Revelation. The ambiguity of what is on the table draws us to note an open space at the table; the circle is not closed. It seems a point of entrance for those who view the icon. The Church is invited to enter into the communion through the Body and Blood of Christ for the life of the world.

In the eucharistic liturgy we celebrate Christ's sacrifice and our life in Christ. To do this well, we employ the full range of our human creativity and ceremonial resourcefulness. As though anticipating our spiritual transformation, we lift up our voices in song. In the presence of Holy Mystery we transform our movements, so that everyday hurrying and scurrying become graceful movement of our bodies. The Book of the Gospels is carried high, raised above every other text, and the gifts of the offering are delivered to the altar in formal procession. We indulge ourselves in other sensory engagement—the scents of wax candles, seasonal flowers and plants, exotic incense. We modify lighting to designate significance, raising candle power or lowering it—even assembling a blaze of lighted tapers. The presence or absence of these ceremonial elements is never to be mistaken for the presence or absence of Holy Mystery during the Church's eucharistic liturgy. We value them in service of the mystery of divine-human communion; they, like we, are "God's humble servants."

The Church Makes the Liturgy;
Worshiping Communities Make the Church

The liturgy is in the books. The liturgy is not in the books. Both statements are true. Let me explain. The Church at Rome publishes official liturgical books. Conferences of Bishops receive those books and confirm with the Roman Church what they judge to be necessary pastoral adjustments. In this magisterial work, there is no negotiation about which relationships are to be celebrated. The faith is one, holy, catholic, and apostolic. The faith is Trinitarian, and it is known to us in the story of Jesus' ministry, dying, and rising.

Still, there have been and can be negotiations about how the mystery is to be understood and lived in the life of the Church. There have been centuries when the eucharistic liturgy was celebrated in the language of the people, centuries when it was celebrated in Latin. There have been centuries when laity communed in both the eucharistic species and centuries when the cup was prohibited. When an early round of postconciliar books were prepared, with the directive that women could serve as lectors, but only while standing outside the sanctuary, the U.S. bishops' conference renegotiated that matter almost immediately. When the revised Funeral Rites were being prepared, a consultation with episcopal conferences led to identification of a widespread pastoral need for prayers for a stillborn infant and for a suicide, neither of which were to be found earlier in the tradition.

Currently the Zaire liturgy, officially approved for parts of what is called "Middle Belt Africa," employs what we call dance, because communal movement is dance and dance is communal movement in these cultures. In one officially authorized setting in India, the eucharistic liturgy is celebrated with the assembly and the priest seated, but sitting is the posture of prayer in their culture.

Bishops deliver the official, yet pastorally adapted, books to the parishes. Only then does the liturgy come off the page and come to life. What is found in the books is brought into action as the liturgical prayer of a local worshiping community. We know from our own experience that not all Catholic liturgies are the same, even when all our parishes are using the same liturgical books. One reason for difference is that the liturgical books themselves provide for choices in some matters. There are practical human reasons for our variety as well, and there are spiritual reasons.

While I know an ecumenical Christian monastic community that has five Julliard-trained organists, this abundance of musical competence is uncommon. Most assemblies come before God as they are in their poverty or their abundance, with the gifts we have been given, not only in the matter of music but in every aspect of our liturgical ministering to one another.

Actual musical ministry, like all aspects of a parish's way of celebrating its Sunday liturgy, gives witness to the historical and cultural traditions of worshiping communities and to socioeconomic matters as well. Faced with these realities, official liturgical books can give warnings about "what not to do." But they cannot take account of local spiritual maturity and Spirit-filled creativity. We know good liturgical keyboarding and bad, good liturgical ensembles and bad, but also good liturgical movement and bad, good processions and bad. In liturgy, the issue of good and bad is not exclusively about skill, although given a choice, skillful is better than skill-less. Whatever is done is to be done at the service of celebrating together the mystery of our faith. Drawing upon the available resources of a community is a genuine liturgical ministry. This ministry is about assisting the assembly in remembering, affirming, and deepening the spiritual relationships that give them their identity.

Yes, the local community celebrating liturgy has official liturgical books among its resources. Yes, it has its human talents and material resources. Then it has its own members, and it has its pastor. Each person comes with personal history, with religious memory, and with religious imagination shaped by the living tradition and by personal life experiences, as well as by contemporary cultural dynamics. Note in this human community the matter of the relative spiritual maturity of the members of the local church. In a parish mix where human egos often grind one another as in a crucible, the Sunday liturgy nevertheless happens. Jesus Christ: yesterday, today, and forever. But we, the beloved community, are fragile, blessed, and broken ourselves. The pain of bringing each idiosyncratic self to the mix is bearable because of the presence of the Holy Spirit comforting and guiding. It is also bearable because of our Spirit-filled memories of deeply moving liturgies that have strengthened and enriched our faith.

In the course of liturgical celebrations of the mystery of faith, each of us learns that the Church, like God, is greater, richer, and deeper, than I can fathom. This depth, richness, and spiritual maturity impresses itself on me. The living tradition of communal worship imprints on me a consciousness of God's mysterious ways that I would never have come to know left to my own personal spiritual quest. Few people once deeply imprinted ever forget completely that their lives are caught up in mystery.

But something else is happening now in our weekly eucharistic celebrations. We are currently experiencing a graced tension and struggle as Church celebrating Eucharist. Local liturgical assemblies are shaping the Catholic tradition, whether by the depth or the superficiality of our ways of remembering and celebrating the Mystery within which we live. When some Catholic communities push back on what the magisterium offers us as the official liturgy—not in adolescent rebellion but on the basis of its spiritual maturing as the ecclesial Body of Christ—the Church itself is being transformed. Consider the matter of women. We have been learning over the course of many years—since Saint Paul wrote of this to the Galatians—that baptized women and men share one identity in Christ. The learning is currently taking place in local struggles about women's liturgical ministries and the language of our public prayer. Women stand among the altar servers and communion ministers in parishes across the country. Gender-inclusive language is being used comfortably and un–self-consciously in parish churches all over the country, both in the proclamation of the Scripture and in the voicing of prayers.

These communal liturgical practices are imprinting on generations young and old an aspect of Christ's work of reconciliation that theological debate alone might never have done. We have not gone the full distance, since we don't know what the full distance is. But a journey has begun toward an as yet uncertain realization of the fullness of the Church's life in Christ.

In recent years some members of the magisterium and some in the local churches have also been "pushing back." In the matter of official liturgical books some—but not all—would have the Church affirm male-gendered language and ministerial practice in the Church's eucharistic celebrations of the mystery of Trinitarian communion. Discerning between human spirits and the Holy Spirit has become part of the challenge of living faithfully with Holy Mystery.

Some Concluding Observations

The speakers who preceded me and who will follow me remind us that the Catholic prayer tradition is wide and varied. The public and communal celebrations of the Catholic people have to be complemented by the other ways we pray as Catholics. Communal spiritual discernment is only possible in a community growing in spiritual maturity. That requires of all of us, whatever our age or ecclesial statures, that we practice the spiritual discipline of quieting ourselves, of entering into interior silence and waiting. What is the Spirit saying to the churches?

Where dioceses and parishes, their leaders and members, are prayerfully waiting for the wisdom that is the gift of the Holy Spirit, there will be fair evidence of this in our liturgical celebrations and in our parish and diocesan life. Again, it is Paul who listed for the Church in Galatians what he named the "fruit of the Spirit…love, joy, peace, patience, kindness, generosity, faithfulness, gentleness, and self-control." As we wait, we trust God to hold us all together within the Mystery of our faith.

5. Prayer and the Coincidence of Opposites

Elizabeth A. Dreyer, Ph.D., Fairfield University

I approach the theme of prayer from the perspective of a "coincidence of opposites." The very foundations of Christianity are built on such coincidences: life comes out of death; the kingdom has come, and yet we pray "Thy kingdom come." In a society that generally values "either-or" over "both-and" thinking, we are partial to answers that come down clearly on one side of an issue or another. This tendency is glaring in students and in literalists, bringing no end of frustration. Legitimate attempts to define or explain something can trap us into putting too much weight on one aspect and underplaying its opposite, thereby obscuring the inherent complexity of existence. Prayer is no exception. I would like to explore the topic of Christian prayer through a series of opposites. Keeping opposites in creative tension is a hallmark of the writings of the Christian mystics. They are superb teachers, whose intense experiences of God lead them to linguistic strategies that both instruct and leave my head spinning.

To begin, let us think of prayer as a constant adventure in relationship with God, as something given to us by God; something we are empowered to do by the Holy Spirit, an articulation of our deepest desires.[1] Prayer is basically gift. What we need to do is relax and consign our anxieties to the Spirit. The goal is simply to pay attention to the prayer that emerges naturally out of the very fiber of our everyday lives. The prayer of each Christian is unique, and yet part of an ages-old communion of saints. Pray the prayer that is given, knowing that at its heart, prayer is in God's hands from

---

1. Simon Tugwell, *Prayer in Practice* (Springfield, IL: Templegate, 1974), 12, 60. See also Thomas Aquinas, *Summa Theologiae* IIa IIae q. 83 a. 1 ad 1.

start to finish.[2] I hope this conference will lead all of us to be more confident and less self-conscious about our prayer.

Each element in the following pairs of opposites is intimately related to the other, and each pair circles around the others—interweaving to create a complex pattern that I believe is ultimately true to our experience of life and of prayer.

What We Know and Don't Know About Prayer

Perhaps the best place to start is simply to come right out with the truth that we don't know what prayer is. This statement does not reflect some brand of false humility. It is the simple, stark truth. If prayer has something to do with the unimaginable, ineffable, wondrous, mysterious Creator of the universe, then it is the case that we do not know anything about it. Paul tells us in Romans: "Likewise the Spirit helps us in our weakness; for we do not know how to pray as we ought, but that very Spirit intercedes with sighs too deep for words. And God, who searches the heart, knows what is the mind of the Spirit, because the Spirit intercedes for the saints according to the will of God" (8:26–27).

But take a look at library or bookstore shelves and notice how many volumes on prayer have been written across the centuries. Pretty impressive. For something we don't know how to do, we sure do a lot of talking and writing about it—and here we are—doing it again! But it is important to take a moment and let the truth that *we don't know how to pray* seep into our deepest consciousness. A range of good effects results. If I don't know how to pray, I am off the hook; likely to listen more; to lean on God more; to be more humble, simple, and realistic. No room for arrogance or false confidence that I know it all.

On the other side of the tension, however, we can rightly say that we *do* know a lot about prayer. The Scriptures tell us about

---

2. Ibid., 9.

prayer; about some of the ways Jesus and his disciples prayed; and the tradition is replete with methods, styles, and nuanced insights about what prayer is and how to do it. Both perspectives are true. We know, speak, write, study, and engage in prayer. And we also don't know what it is or how to do it.

God Immanent and Transcendent

Now that we have ascertained that we do not know how to pray, let us spend the rest of our time together talking about how to do it. The backdrop for prayer—including conscious and unconscious elements—is God and our image of God. Our ideas about God come from many places—family, education, church, and society. It is an instructive exercise to jot down the image of God you think you have, and the image of God who is actually operative in your prayer. You may say that God is kind and loving, but you may pray like God is a fearful ogre, a distant relative, or a disinterested bystander. Our prayer depends on our operative images of God.

Images of God are generally categorized as transcendent and immanent. Some of us see and experience God as awesome and powerful, that than which nothing greater can be thought, to cite Saint Anselm. How is it even possible to find language for this overwhelmingly mysterious, utterly transcendent God? Catherine of Siena puts it quite dramatically. She says to God: "You are. I am not."[3] This is not something she read in a textbook, but something she discovered in the depths of her prayer. She saw the majesty of God and in comparison, judged herself, rightly, to be nothing. This is the feeling referred to by Rudolph Otto's description of God as *mysterium fascinans et tremendum;* it lies behind the many case studies in William James's *Varieties of Religious Experience.*

Our images of God can be personal or impersonal—God is my

---

3. See Elizabeth A. Dreyer, *A Retreat With Catherine of Siena* (Cincinnati: St. Anthony Messenger Press, 1999).

rock, my fortress, my deliverer. From the world of science, we borrow language to describe God as a force field or the swirling patterns of stars and galaxies. We may see God's power as power "over" us, or we may see it as relational power—a power that engages in creation and history and desires our well-being in every way. One sure source for understanding the truth of God's power is the cross, the place where God chose to abandon divine power and die out of love.[4]

At the same time, we experience God as so close that words escape us again. What can it possibly mean that God is closer to us than we are to ourselves? For some, God is a constant friend; for others a lover; for yet others, a genial companion. The mystics are the models *par excellence* of human beings who allow themselves to enter into a most intimate relationship with God. Some turn to the *Song of Songs* to speak about this love affair, using erotic, sexual imagery to capture this most intimate of relationships. They, above all others, teach us about a God who relates to us in a very horizontal way. But they never let go of the vertical pole; they never forget that God is awesome Creator of the universe.

Each of us may have a God who tends more toward the transcendent or the immanent. This is as it should be. As you well know, our images of God change as we develop and grow as human beings. What worked at twenty may bore us to death at thirty, become inadequate at forty, puzzling at fifty, funny at sixty. It is important to be open to these differences and developments. God is better accounted for by "both-and." We should resist the temptation to drop one side of the equation.

Privilege and Duty

When we turn from the divine to the human side, we encounter another range of opposites. One involves the privilege of prayer ver-

---

4. See Elizabeth A. Dreyer, *The Cross in Christian Tradition: From Paul to Bonaventure* (New York and Mahwah, NJ: Paulist Press, 2000).

sus the duty of prayer. Some authors rightly remind us that we pray because we have been told to. Paul tells the community to rejoice always, pray constantly, and give thanks in all circumstances (see 1 Thessalonians 5:16–18). Prayer is a command, a duty, a responsibility, not an option. This is good advice. When life gets sticky or downright depressing, when we find ourselves between a rock and a hard place, it can be helpful to pray simply because God commands it. But there is an exquisite tension between following orders and realizing that we have a God who *wants* to talk with us and *wants* us to talk back, a God who has told us that the divine happiness depends on our prayerful, mutual presence, a God whose deepest desire is self-communication. "What are human beings that you are mindful of them, mortals that you care for them?" (Psalm 8:4). What enormous privilege to be invited by the Creator, Healer, and Comforter to engage in intimate conversation and presence.

The eucharistic prayer in the Congregational liturgy has the following line: "we come to the table, not because we must, but because we may." In our culture, it is not easy to feel a humble sense of privilege. More common is a sense of entitlement—life is "owed" me—a house, car, education, food, entertainment, lots of technological gadgets, marble countertops, fancy appliances, fashionable clothes, the opportunity to travel. Experiencing the invitation to prayer is an effective antidote to our sense of entitlement. "Be still and know that I am God!" (Psalm 46:10). We enter into the chamber of the bridegroom with humility and awe and thanks.

Silent, Vocal, Bodily Prayer

Mental prayer may be the most common form of prayer. Prayer is mental when thoughts or words come into consciousness; when we offer petitions or ejaculations to God. Singing is another form of vocal prayer—to pray twice, as the saying goes. We usually engage in vocal prayer before meals, in prayer groups, or in public liturgical settings. But as central to prayer as words are, they are not our only alternative. The practice of centering prayer may involve the gentle repetition of a single word, or mantra, to keep our attention focused on communion with God. In other forms of prayer the goal is to eliminate all words and images. We simply sit in the silence of God-with-us. Saint Augustine reminds us that "in most cases prayer consists more in groaning than in speaking, in tears rather than in words." But God sees our tears, and our "groaning is not hidden from a God who made all things by the word, and does not need human words."[5]

Heart and intention are key to prayer, and Thomas Aquinas wisely reminds us that when we get bored in prayer, it is time to stop.[6] Our relationship with God should not be characterized as enforced interaction, nor as an artificial "construct" that is divorced from who we truly are. Genuine prayer is part of the warp and woof of our real, messy, but glorious existence.

Unfortunately, in all these forms of prayer, we are not likely to pay much attention to our bodies. There is some bodily gesture in liturgy, but in our private prayer, we might consider prayer in which we walk or run, or drive; lay on the floor, dance, or engage in various body movements such as yoga or stretching. There is no "recipe" for bodily involvement in prayer. Many of our ancestors in the faith prayed out loud with hands outstretched or prostrate on the ground. The point is to get confident and comfortable enough to experiment, to find ways to use our bodies to feed our relationship with God in constructive ways.

Long/Big/Complex and Short/Small/Simple Prayer

Sometimes we engage in "big" prayer—praying for peace, or healing for a troubled world. There is also extended prayer: a thirty-day

---

5. Augustine: Letter 130.x.20.

6. *Summa theologiae* IIa IIae q. 83 a. 14. Cited in Simon Tugwell, *Prayer in Practice*, 10–11.

retreat, the Easter Triduum, or simply Sunday worship for some Orthodox or African-American Christians. When this type of prayer is given, we should go with it. But for most of us, prayer probably revolves around smaller, even trivial, daily affairs. Some of us may choose to carve out a half hour to pray each day. More likely, we pray short prayers strung like a ribbon throughout the day.

I agree that very frequent, short prayer may be the best kind of prayer. The seventeenth-century Carmelite, Brother Lawrence of the Resurrection, left a legacy he called "The Practice of the Presence of God." Jesuit Jean-Pierre de Caussade instructs us in what he calls "The Sacrament of the Present Moment." Ignatius of Loyola reminds us to "find God in all things." Our contemporary, Bill Callahan, calls this type of prayer "noisy contemplation."[7] Prayer in any given day might range from "help!" to "thanks," to "catch you later," to "where are you?", to "please help Sammy get through this," to "whoopee!", to "God, you are great!"

Implicit and Explicit Prayer

It may also be helpful to make a distinction between explicit and implicit prayer. When we think about prayer, generally what comes to mind is *explicit prayer*. This is prayer that looks, tastes, smells, and feels like what we think of as "the sacred"—grace before meals, Sunday liturgy, morning and evening prayers, ejaculations, retreats, volunteering at a shelter or food program. These are important moments of prayer, but in terms of time in a week, the average person is likely to be engaged in explicit prayer infrequently.

During the greater part of our days and nights, most of us engage in *implicit prayer*—raising kids; going to the office; attending school

---

7. Jean-Pierre de Caussade, *The Sacrament of the Present Moment* (San Francisco: Harper, 1966); Brother Lawrence of the Resurrection, *The Practice of the Presence of God* (Boston: New Seeds, 2005); Ignatius of Loyola, *The Spiritual Exercises* (Chicago: Loyola University Press, 1951); William Callahan, *Noisy Contemplation: Deep Prayer for Busy People* (Hyattsville, MD: The Quixote Center, 1994).

board meetings and parent conferences; entertaining friends; playing chauffeur for sports events and music lessons; going to school, or a concert, or a basketball game; getting a few hours of sleep. On the surface, these activities look and feel like no more than that—the ordinary round of things we do each day. What makes them prayer is what I call "structures of meaning." Changing a diaper can be prayer because I have done something with my consciousness, my intention to make it so.

How do I do this? Aiming to fulfill the command of 1 Thessalonians—"Pray without ceasing" (5:17)—I have a desire, I make a decision to change ordinary acts into acts of prayer. I may simply offer my day when I open my eyes in the morning by praying the Morning Offering. "Everything I do today is yours, O God. Take and receive." Making everything I do prayer also depends on moments of explicit prayer. From time to time, I need to step away, become quiet, go on a retreat, take a walk by myself in which I formally reconnect with God and renew my desire and my decision that I want every aspect of my life to be related to prayer.

But opportunities for implicit prayer are legion. Turning on the hot water tap in the shower can symbolize the rushing, cleansing, healing outpouring of the Holy Spirit into our hearts (see Romans 5:5). Acknowledging the presence of a family member as he or she enters the room is a gesture that offers up, consecrates, honors the sacredness of this person's existence. Gritting my teeth and keeping my mouth shut, speaking the truth in difficult circumstances, exercising tolerance and patience when I am ready to kill a family member or neighbor or coworker, resisting road rage, offering a kind word instead of keeping silent or being critical—all of these moments are potentially prayer.

A set of opposites related to explicit/implicit prayer is prayer that is extrinsic or intrinsic. The idea of *extrinsic* grace or prayer is out of favor these days because it is seen as something outside of us, something added on, rather than integral to our existence.

Theologians tell us that if we are to take the Incarnation seriously, then we have to admit that every molecule and subatomic particle has been blessed and made sacred through Jesus' presence among us. Grace is not like the head on a beer, or the frosting on a cake, but an integral part of the beer and cake.

If we acknowledge the *intrinsic* change in reality brought about by the Incarnation, then our usual categories of sacred and secular require significant adjustment. I would like to take as an example the dinner tables that most of us have in our homes or apartments. When we gather around a table with our families or friends, in what sense is this Eucharist? In what sense is this prayer? I am sympathetic with Karl Rahner's idea of the cosmic liturgy in which the primordial act of praise and thanksgiving takes place in the universe and only secondarily at the formal sacrament. These two loci of God's activity are both important and mutually enrich each other, but Rahner reminds us that God acts, above all, in the world. The formal sacraments are derivative, effecting a divine presence that points to the larger, cosmic liturgy.

How many of us understand what we do at our dinner tables as genuinely, intrinsically eucharistic—even when there are babies throwing food and teen-agers fighting? Dinner in our homes is not something extrinsic, or extra, or reflective of something else. Breaking bread together, welcoming friend and stranger, enjoying the pleasure of each other's company, engaging in conversation, enduring the tension of discord or the cacophony of children, struggling to be present to each other when our schedules take us in different directions—this is "real" Eucharist. This event that takes place daily is an occasion of prayer when we offer ourselves and each other to God, when we are present to each other in love and struggle, when we are mindful of those who are without food, when we praise and gives thanks to a generous and loving God. We can choose to pray no matter what is going on in our lives. The *meaning* of our dining room tables can make it just another dinner, or a time of connection or struggle with each other and God. Our theology supports us in this desire to relate every part of our lives to God.

Prayer: Ordinary, Intimate, and the Dark

Prayer is easy and enjoyable when it is going well, when God seems to be listening, and responding, to our prayer. We might call this the *prayer of light*. We are connecting with God. The conversation is engaging. New insights appear. Feelings of "consolation" are present. God is good, the world is manageable, we feel like we grasp what prayer is all about, and we experience gratitude to be in relationship with God. We pray at liturgy, at home, at work, on an occasional retreat without incident or crisis. We don't think about it too much, because it seems to be going along fine. Ordinary prayer is a gift and we should not minimize, much less disdain it.

This type of prayer does not necessarily take God for granted. On the one hand, life cannot bear too much intensity, so most of the time, we relate to God in a relaxed "everyday" kind of way. But if it goes on forever, and becomes the only way we pray, we can become lulled into complacency or seduced by mediocrity. This is what Teresa of Ávila describes in the Third Mansion of her *Interior Castle*. A very honest student in one of my classes at the seminary who was preparing for ministry suggested that this is the plateau many people in Christian churches reach and in which they stall out. This is the moment, says Teresa, to stick with the program and open ourselves to greater gifts. Don't get lulled into thinking that this is all God has in store for us, because there is so much more that is possible. Imagination plays an important role here. "What no eye has seen, nor ear heard, nor the human heart conceived, what God has prepared for those who love him"—these things God has revealed to us through the Spirit (1 Corinthians 2:9–10).

Others reach a point at which prayer brings friction rather than comfort. We become edgy, discontent in prayer. Thomas Merton uses the metaphor of one's dwelling to describe this state of affairs.

We go along pleased with the way we have arranged the furniture of our lives. It is pleasant, familiar; we are content. But then one day, you walk into the room of your life and everything is wrong. The colors no longer work; the furniture and paintings look ugly and irritate. This moment, he says, can be a call to conversion, to go deeper. And while it is understandable and acceptable to have to rearrange the furniture of our lives at twenty or thirty, it gets downright inconvenient and embarrassing when it happens at fifty or sixty or even seventy. But if we respond to the upset, which Merton says is like going through adolescence again (heaven forbid!), we will again find a rhythm of prayer that will bring comfort and stability, until the next remodeling job is called for.

There are still other times—what John of the Cross describes as the "dark night of the soul"—when our minds and senses are stripped. God is silent, absent, removed, seemingly indifferent. We don't have a clue about what is going on in our prayer. We can't or won't even try to pray. Many pundits characterize postmodern culture as a time of God's absence. Much twentieth-century art, literature, and film reflects the feeling that God has abandoned us, withdrawn from human intercourse. The chilling films of Ingmar Bergman or "Death of God" theology come to mind.

How are we to respond to the perception that God has become silent? Perhaps this absent God is partially behind the enormous growth of the Pentecostal movement. The rituals, traditions, and prayer practices of this branch of the Christian family surely signal that God is still alive and well in our midst, bestowing the Spirit's gifts in abundance.[8] Another response to God's absence is fundamentalism, which sees human behavior as the cause for God's

---

8. In 1977, Kansas City was the site for an international "general conference" of all charismatics and Pentecostals, bringing together all the sectors of the renewal for the first time. The purpose was to demonstrate the movement's unity and to make a "common witness" to the church and the world of the conference theme, "Jesus Is Lord."

withdrawal. A strict return to an absolute certainty and literalism in biblical interpretation and spiritual practices are aimed at convincing God to join us once again.

Darkness in prayer calls for a steady will. It demands that we show up for prayer, not because it is rewarding or feels good, or helps us in our lives—because it doesn't anymore—but simply as an act of desire. At these moments, we decide to remain loyal to God. We may sit for a few moments without energy, feeling, or grace; dumb and numb. Yet, we continue to offer ourselves to God each day. Gregory of Nyssa writes movingly about the power of desire that leads us to want God no matter what kind of return I am getting from the relationship. Even if God never seems to show up, what a great life it would be to have spent it simply wanting God. God loves a generous giver, but generosity is challenged when prayer goes dead. And yet we are free to choose to show up anyway.

John of the Cross lays out a challenging path that involves acceptance of the dryness of prayer; hope that there is light at the end of the tunnel; trust and confidence that God will lead us through the darkness to a kind of joy, love, and happiness that is infinitely better than what we knew before the darkness. Contemplative Carmelite Constance Fitzgerald wrote a wonderful article, "Impasse and Dark Night," about this process that involves turning ourselves over to right-brain processes that transcend reason and "figuring out" what is going on.[9] Experiencing God as silent or absent can take place in life as well as prayer: the stripping that routinely accompanies family and work life; children who are bored, addicted, or indifferent to others' well-being; impossible, bruising work situations; illnesses that take an enormous toll on us and our loved ones; the aging pro-

---

9. Constance Fitzgerald, "Impasse and Dark Night" in *Women's Spirituality: Resources for Christian Development,* ed., Joann Wolski Conn, 2nd ed. (New York and Mahwah, NJ: Paulist Press, 1996), 410–35; and *Living with Apocalypse, Spiritual Resources for Social Compassion* (San Francisco: Harper & Row, 1984), 93–116; http://www.geocities.com/baltimorecarmel/johncross/impasse.html.

cess during which we may lose our hearing, sight, ability to walk or think or recognize others. Each of these examples of suffering—the breadth and depth of which reaches across the globe in ways too horrendous to contemplate—is a chance for heroic prayer.

In both the ordinariness and the darkness of prayer, it is important to keep ourselves open to something different, to imagine more rather than less. Throughout the tradition, laity have been viewed almost exclusively in terms of the lower levels of prayer. Today, after Vatican II and its emphasis on the universal, baptismal call to holiness, we no longer see ourselves as second-class citizens when it comes to prayer and holiness. We are challenged to "try on" the image of God as intimate lover or friend.

Twelfth-century Cistercian abbot, Bernard of Clairvaux, is famous for his sermons on the *Song of Songs* in which he encourages the monks to become lovers of God in Christ. Thirteenth-century Beguine, Hadewijch of Brabant, speaks of her relationship with God in terms of erotic images and metaphors that reflect the intimacy of a love affair.[10] However we think about the more intense, usually fleeting, mystical reaches of prayer, we are wise to leave ourselves open to this possibility. Each, in her or his own way, is invited to "go for the gold," to ascend to the mountaintop, to enter into a relationship of transfiguration with God.

Gift/Passive and Work/Active

Another set of opposites points to prayer as gift and prayer as work. At its most profound level, prayer is gift. It is a great blessing when this knowledge washes over us and we experience the pure gratuitousness of standing in God's presence. We do nothing. God does all. But learning the techniques of prayer is work; it takes time and

---

10. See Elizabeth A. Dreyer, *Passionate Spirituality: Hildegard of Bingen and Hadewijch of Brabant* (Mahwah, NJ: Paulist Press, 2005). See also *Earth Crammed With Heaven: A Spirituality of Everyday Life* (Mahwah, NJ: Paulist Press, 1994).

energy and commitment to find ways to have my entire life be a life of prayer. Rather than parsing out percentages, I like to think of prayer as 100% God's efforts and 100% our own. The rhythms of our lives move from periods in which we are sweating with the effort to be prayerful (the fourteenth-century anonymous text *The Cloud of Unknowing* is a good example), to times we are swept up to the seventh heaven in a moment of ecstasy that is unplanned, unprepared for, undeserved.

We need both deep prayer and techniques. When we reflect on certain moments in our love relationships, we get a glimpse of the effortless, spontaneous feelings and actions that develop in a very deep place within our being. Our responses emerge naturally out of the truth that we are in love. In prayer, when our hearts have been transformed from stone to flesh, we are called from deep to deep. This connection is experienced as pure gift. It might be a moment, like one I had recently holding our first grandchild in my arms. The utter beauty and joy of this touch turned into a prayer in which the ego was abandoned without any effort as I crossed over into blessing this child and his parents. Or it might take place in nature—walking a beach, wandering through a forest, the first snowfall, watching a bird soar through the sky, weeping at the beauty of the Grand Canyon or the Rocky Mountains. Or this intense experience may happen in a quiet moment of prayer when we let our spirits soar to become one with the Holy Spirit of joy, grace, and freedom.

Some who know this kind of prayer say it is not possible to teach prayer. It is a gift and you either have it or you don't. At some level, this sentiment has a grain of truth in it, but it misses a larger truth. We are not born knowing how to pray, and patterns or methods of prayer can indeed be taught. To teach methods in prayer does not mean that we intend to coerce God's presence. On the contrary, learning about prayer gives us the tools to prepare ourselves, to get ready for the gift of God's presence in good times and bad.

Conclusion: Tradition and My Particular Way

The Catholic tradition offers us so much help in the area of prayer that it is downright embarrassing. From this storehouse, all of us can find a way of prayer that fits our particular personality and context. It is a tragedy if we do not know, treasure, and use this heritage in creative and critical ways. It is often necessary to translate a mostly monastic tradition into the lifestyles of active laypersons. The tradition is not perfect—there are aspects of the past that we are wise to leave behind. But overall, it is our responsibility and privilege to keep this tradition of prayer alive and well by interpreting it, allowing it to judge us, adapting it, testing it against the realities of our lives in the twenty-first–century global village in which we live. We should never think about our prayer outside the context of our entire life in all its particularity and change. The buck stops with us individually and communally. Our job is to take prayer seriously, to desire it, to do it.

It is also our job to experiment, sift, and stick with it so that we will continue at each stage of our lives to find the truest and most practical way of making our lives prayerful. Each path will be unique. At times help may be ready at hand; at other times, we may have to go it alone. In either case, our capacity for God—the call to become holy like God—is perhaps the most astonishing thing about a life of faith. The journey invites us to keep opposites in creative tension, to engage in all the dimensions of prayer and in all kinds of prayer—praise, lament, petition, thanksgiving, silence. We pray alone and with others—from local faith communities to the communion of saints. We are asked to discover our strengths and preferences in prayer and be mindful of keeping our prayer simple, lively, and committed. And we must remember the advice of the fifth-century monk, Cassian, who reminded us that our best prayer may take place when we are unaware that we are praying.[11]

---

11. Cassian, *Conferences*, IX, 31.

I close with a citation from the German Jesuit theologian Karl Rahner (d. 1984) about grace, the heart of prayer. He suggests that grace [prayer] is

> ...*simply the ultimate depth of everything spiritual creatures do when they realize themselves—when one laughs and cries, accepts responsibility, loves, lives and dies, stands up for truth, breaks out of preoccupation with self to help the neighbor, hopes against hope, cheerfully refuses to be embittered by the stupidity of daily life, keeps silent not so that evil festers in our hearts but so that it dies there—when in a word, one lives as one would like to live, in opposition to selfishness and to the despair that always assails us. This is where grace occurs, because all this leads humans into the infinity and victory that is God.*[12]

---

12. Karl Rahner, "How to Receive a Sacrament and Mean It," *Theology Digest* 19 (Autumn 1971): 227–34.

6. Prayer and Decision-Making

Most Reverend Raymond J. Boland, D.D.,
Bishop Emeritus, Diocese of Kansas City-St. Joseph

In searching for a theme for my talk I came across that oft-quoted piece of sage advice which has its roots in Jewish literature. The author, whoever he or she was, put it this way:

> *"pray as if everything depended on God,*
> *act as if everything depended on you."*

One may think this "catch phrase" somewhat trite, but the interdependency which is expressed is most important when it comes to decision-making and leadership. Long before we are moved to turn to God in prayer—which most would agree is in itself a grace from God—he endowed us with many human abilities and aspirations that are reflective of the love by which we are fashioned in his image and likeness. There is a symphony of creation expressed in Genesis which culminates in an extraordinary divine-human relationship which, by its very nature, necessitates intercommunication or what we like to call *prayer*. Those "made a little less than the angels" (Psalm 8:5) are recipients of the divine adoption proclaimed by Ezekiel, "you will be my people and I will be your God" (Ezekiel 36:28). The devastating Hurricane Katrina revivified and updated an old story that illustrates this point. As the water began to rise along his street, a man of deep faith got down on his knees and asked God to save him. The police came by and asked him to evacuate his house, but he assured them that God would take care of him. The waters continued to rise and he continued to pray, now on the second floor. A boat on a rescue detail pulled under his window and offered him a ride. Once again he declined and he resumed his prayers. Some hours later, now on his rooftop, he waved away an Air Force helicopter as it prepared to lower a rescue basket. "God will take care of me," he shouted above the noise of the engine and the storm. During the night he drowned and upon arrival at the Pearly Gates angrily demanded to know why God had not responded to his prayers. God replied, "Who do you think sent the police and the Marines and the helicopter?" Now, we know that nothing is impossible for God, but we also know that a healthy belief in miracles includes acceptance of the principle that they are not to be multiplied without necessity.

Let me propose one other preliminary point for your reflection. We must never underestimate the significance of the Incarnation in the enrichment of our prayer lives. When God became human, the whole dynamic changed. More than once we are assured in the sacred narratives that Christ became one of us in every way with the exception of sin (see Hebrews 4:15–16 and Philippians 2:6–8.). Without in any way lessening our belief in his divinity, I would submit that it is easier for most of us to build up a relationship with somebody who shares our humanity. After all, such relationships, on another level, are the components of daily living. The Incarnation, a vital part of God's salvific plan for our redemption, is also the great gift which God gives us to reduce the distance, as it were, between an incomprehensible Absolute Infinity and the God-man Christ who wishes us to be his brothers and sisters. This statement may be an overly broad generalization and we must be careful to avoid, as Karl Rahner advises us, the risk "of reducing the divine person to the level of other beings" or promoting an encounter no more substantial than an exercise in pious sentimentality.[1]

When it comes to decision-making and when it comes to prayer,

---

1. Karl Rahner, *Encyclopedia of Theology: The* Concise Sacramentum Mundi (New York: Seabury Press, 1975), 1268:1.

I believe we can have no greater exemplar than Christ himself. A few careful readings of the gospels will readily convince us that Christ was a man of prayer living in constant communion with the Father and pulsating with the power of the Spirit, that mysterious inner life of the Trinity. This does not surprise us. What is remarkable, however, is that his apostles, who, right up to the very end had difficulties in comprehending the purpose of the Lord's mission, had no difficulty in noticing the value of his prayer life. They envied him and openly sought his instruction, "Lord, teach us to pray...." (Luke 11:1) What is also remarkable is that the four evangelists thought it important to record that Christ prayed more seriously and more ardently before he made his decisions of consequence. Intellectually acknowledging the premise that an all-powerful God did not need to pray before making any decision, we can only conclude that at least one of his reasons was to give us an example. Allow me to mention and comment on a few of the most obvious instances.

When Christ decided that the time had come to begin his public ministry, he entered the desert for what in effect was a forty-day retreat. In many ways the temptations he resisted honed his personality to become the living embodiment of the Beatitudes, which he subsequently proclaimed and which are gathered together for us by Matthew in what we have come to know as the Sermon on the Mount (see Matthew 5:1–12). This experience—allied with the dramatic announcement of his mission, with its Isaian overtones, at the Sabbath prayer service in Nazareth's synagogue—set in motion a three-year pilgrimage that would culminate with his crucifixion outside the city wall of Jerusalem.

His next great decision was the selection of his coworkers. We are told that he spent the entire night in prayer before he named the twelve (see Luke 6:12; Mark 3:13–19), by all accounts a motley group which, intriguingly, included one who would be forever remembered as his betrayer. Is there a lesson for us here and, if so, what is it? Then there is his concern for his chosen vicar, the impetuous Peter. Christ prays that his faith will not fail (Luke 22:32) and as he knows the end is drawing nigh, he pours out his heart in prayer that all may be one, "as you, Father, are in me, and I am in you" (John 17:21). There are a multitude of incidents in the gospels where Christ enfolded his decisions in the context of prayer. I can only recommend that you reread and ponder once again the episode known as the Transfiguration, his presence at Cana, the restoration of Lazarus to life, and his gifting of the Eucharist.

It is impossible to comprehend the depth of his prayer when he decided to embrace his passion and the cross, "a death which he freely accepted," as we say in the Second Eucharistic Prayer. In agony, in Gethsemane, "Father, if you are willing, remove this cup from me; yet, not my will but yours be done" (Luke 22:42). Here we have petition and submission, qualities that always go together in genuine prayer. A few hours later, as the sacrifice neared completion, as his life ebbed away, "Father, forgive them; for they do not know what they are doing"(Luke 23:24), followed by "My God, my God, why have you forsaken me?" (Mark 15:34), to be capped by "Father, into your hands I commend my spirit" (Luke 23:46), this last being the final affirmation of his life of prayer.

Christ carried the burden and the joy and the achievement of the redemption on his shoulders and he is naturally the one we need to imitate. Among his antecedents and his followers, however, you will find many who crafted lives of holiness and integrity and love by consistently making decisions within the context of their faith expressed in prayer. We call them "saints" and not all of them have been canonized. Maybe you know a few who taught you how to pray, just as Mary and Joseph opened the mind and heart of Jesus to the Father while at the same time struggling to understand the true identity of the child committed to their care.

Now, my thesis is a simple one. I believe that if Christ resorted to prayer in a very special way before he made his important decisions, then we should do the same. In many ways this is a no-brainer. In everyday life we do it all the time. When the even tenor of our ways is suddenly disrupted by crisis, distress, panic, unexpected loss, stubborn dilemmas, or bad news with potentially serious implications, we cry for help and it is only natural for the person of faith to turn to God. Indeed, on such occasions I have known atheists to turn to the God they don't believe in, although I suspect they are more inclined to want to make a deal! We can consider decision-making under two headings—those that tend to be strictly personal and those that involve the welfare of others. These are not mutually exclusive as it is reasonable to expect that the kind of person one is or becomes should influence what he does. Unfortunately, the linkage between one's convictions and one's behavior can be ignored, and we have witnessed sad instances of this in recent years both in the Church and public life.

In the belief that the experiences of one person, namely myself, can be reflective of the experiences of many, let me share some incidents in my own life where I found prayer to be more than consequential when I came to a fork in the road and a decision had to be made. I am not entirely comfortable in using myself as an example as such trips down memory lane can be maudlin in the extreme. I hope you can figure out the parallels in your own life experiences. So, here goes.

My decision to become a priest required prayer. I was not one of those blessed souls who knew from the age of seven that he would be a priest someday. There were other attractive options that required serious consideration. That decision made, I felt called to volunteer my services as a priest to some overseas diocese where there was a shortage of clergy. I entered All Hallows Missionary College in Dublin, which only prepared priests for overseas dioceses, specifically for those countries to which the Irish had emigrated in such large numbers during the Great Famine of the mid-1800s.

My next dilemma was where to go. I was offered four dioceses—

Sydney and Maitland in Australia and Spokane and Washington, D.C., here in the United States. Prayer reconciled my mind to accepting the one that first accepted me. The mail from Washington, D.C., was the fastest. My next challenge, which necessitated more prayer than usual, came six years later when I rejected an invitation from my local bishop in Cork to join my home diocese. I pleaded my many-years' commitment to Washington and he agreed with me. Then came ordination, adaptation to another culture, citizenship, and the heady days of the Second Vatican Council. These events were followed by crisis and the need for prayer as never before—for guidance, survival, perseverance. It was 1967 and for diverse reasons a major confrontation broke out between Archbishop O'Boyle and a large number of our priests. Some of the brightest and best, many of them my close friends, said goodbye to the priesthood and the exodus never seemed to stop. Morale among the priests was abysmal. Those of us who stayed were accused of not having the courage to leave. The crisis passed but the scars remained.

To make my point, let me give you two more examples to complete this egotistical merry-go-round.

On the day I was informed that I was to be the Bishop of Birmingham, my whole little world came tumbling down: I couldn't eat, I couldn't sleep and, believe it or not, I could hardly speak! Ironically, in secular professions such a promotion, and I suppose becoming a bishop could be ranked as a promotion, would justify a sense of achievement and bring out the champagne bottles. I cannot envisage a new senator, a new four-star general, a new judge, a new CEO, or even the winner of "Star Search" doing anything other than hugging the limelight. But here I was, overwhelmed by the enormity of the pastoral challenge of the episcopacy literally running for cover. My comfort zone was shattered. My refuge became one of the chapels in the National Shrine of the Immaculate Conception and my sojourn there, along with the calm measured advice of my then-boss, Archbishop Hickey, convinced me to believe in the power of sacramental grace. It was reminiscent of the dialogue of Paul and Timothy in another century.

Then came 1997 and a diagnosis of colon cancer. Cancer has a powerful way of disrupting one's lifestyle akin to running at full throttle into a brick wall. Suddenly a lot of important activities lost their importance and the concept of mortality took center stage. I prayed, probably selfishly (I know selfishly), and this time I was aware of the prayers of so many others on my behalf as I drifted in and out of that strange morphine-induced nirvana of the postsurgery patient. I recollected the Gaelic prayers of my childhood, "Is giorra cabhir Dé ná an doras" (God's help is closer than the door), and the rather cryptic plea, "may the Lord take a liking to you but not too soon!" And, let me add, never underestimate the spiritual tonic of the sacrament of the sick.

Now, I have shared some of the critical junctures in my life where decision-making and prayer went hand in hand on a personal level. Each one of you could do the same but, rest assured, I am not going to ask anyone to come up here to give witness to similar memorable life experiences. I do recommend, however, that in addition to your regular pattern of prayer-intimacy with God that you seek a more goal-oriented dialogue with him every time you have to make a serious decision. May I be stronger? For a person of faith, it should be an imperative, not an option. An old beer commercial reminds us that "we only go round once in life," and granted that we will all make mistakes, it is vitally important that we beg God, in his goodness, to help us avoid the really serious ones, the ones that may change our lives irreparably. Here is a listing of some of those areas where human happiness may depend on the alignment of our desires with God's will: selecting a career in life; the search for a life partner; preparing for one's marriage commitment; the challenge of raising children successfully; getting one's priorities in order; taking a stand for morality and justice; resisting the temptation to take the easy way out often disguised by the excuse that it's not my responsibility anyway; working in a profession that is inherently dangerous; dealing with one's elderly relatives or the disabilities of personal aging; accepting the loss of a spouse, a child, or a job; coping with illness, both physical and mental; and those myriad unexpected crisis of various proportions when you realize that "the sky is falling" and "the wheels are coming off."

In the course of human events, some people attain positions where their decisions profoundly impact the lives of others. Bishops are in that category, but time precludes me from mentioning those responsibilities of this bishop where prayer was absolutely necessary. Prayer includes discernment with others and it nurtures one's style of leadership. One needs it for teaching, in preparing homilies, in guiding personnel, in the empowerment of others so that in their ministries they too become leaders of prayer. In the Birmingham diocese we had to deal with the murder of a priest, a gut-wrenching experience for any bishop akin to what Abbot Gregory faced so pastorally when a crazed gunman killed two of his monks within the monastery. Then there were decisions dealing with the sex abuse crisis and the more mundane challenge of building churches and schools for the twenty-first century. In his prayer, a bishop has to respect the past, act in the present, and plan for the future, allowing God to be part of the solution and depending on him for support. Besides bishops there are also politicians, CEOs, teachers, doctors, lawyers, pharmacists, parents, youth leaders, military personnel, members of the media, and I could go on and on. This list is not synonymous with the Litany of the Saints. The seven deadly sins are alive and well in our culture as the words "sex abuse crisis," "Enron," "Abugrade Prison," and "abortion statistics" conjure up images of trust violated, greed triumphant, responsibility abdicated, and morality ditched in favor of expediency. The sad commentary is that most of these people would call themselves Christians. Is there an answer? Although specifically addressing those who are engaged in charitable work, the recommendation of Pope Benedict XVI in his first encyclical, *Deus Caritas Est* (God is Love) would apply to all leaders and decision-makers who populate our Church and the body politic. Paragraph 37 of the papal letter reads:

> *It is time to reaffirm the importance of prayer in the face of the activism and the growing secularism of many Christians.... Clearly, the Christian who prays does not claim to be able to change God's plans or correct what he has foreseen. Rather, he seeks an encounter with the Father of Jesus Christ, asking God to be present with the consolation of the Spirit to him and his work. A personal relationship with God and an abandonment to his will can prevent man from being demeaned and save him from falling prey to the teaching of fanaticism and terrorism. An authentically religious attitude prevents man from presuming to judge God.... When people claim to build a case against God in defense of man, on whom can they depend when human activity proves powerless?*

When we pray about our decisions, especially those which impact others, there is a greater likelihood that wisdom will trump caprice, Christian courtesy will calm controversy, service will soften authority, and generous compliance will nurture growth.

When all is said and done, we must never forget that prayer is not a pleasant or even despairing conversation between two very fallible and trouble-prone individuals. No, the one on the other side is the God-Father in the best sense of that combination of words. He loves us even when we are particularly unlovable. He is compassionate when we stray. He is patient when we try to run away. Can I surmise that he must be mightily amused when we play our self-righteous games? Remember the adage with which I began:

> *Pray as if everything depended on God,*
> *act as if everything depended on you.*

I know it may not be easy for control freaks or those who have been diagnosed as having Type-A personalities, not too dissimilar from the disease of self-sufficiency, but I like the advice of Don Helder Câmara, the great champion of the poor and revered as the saintly archbishop of Olinda in Brazil. He tells us about God, "accept surprises that upset your plans, shatter your dreams, give a completely different turn to your day and…who knows…to your life? It is not chance. Leave the Father free to weave the pattern of your days."

This immigrant priest could never have predicted a pilgrimage of service from Cork to Washington to Birmingham and finally to Kansas City. It has been quite a ride and I have loved every moment of it. What can I say except, thank you, God.

Panel Discussion

Richard Miller: We will begin with a question for Sr. Bergant and Dr. Calef: How to reconcile complaint with not blaming God for bad things? So how do we reconcile complaint or complaining to God if not blaming God for bad things?

Dianne Bergant: To answer that question from the context of the psalms, there is no difference, no need to reconcile because when you complain to God, you're blaming God. I mean that's precisely what the psalmist is doing, so I don't know if the question being asked is how do *we* reconcile it, or how does the *psalm* reconcile it. So from the perspective of the psalms, when they are saying, "You did this. Why did you do that?" Well, I think that's blaming. Now from our perspective, the best that theology can do is try to be accurate. Theology will never be adequate. So you say one thing with an approximation of accuracy, you don't say something else. Now, having said that, if we believe that God is in charge of everything, and theology says there is either what they say is the *explicit* will of God or the *permissive* will of God, which means God either explicitly does it or allows it to be done, then once again—I hope this does not sound cold and heartless—and I do not believe it sounds blasphemous—there is very little difference between complaining to God and blaming God because if God is in charge, well, then somehow or other God is responsible. That's the short answer.

Richard Miller: This is for everyone: To say that prayers are unanswered, does that mean first that they are not worthy or of value? Or that God heard but said "no"? Or the person who is praying is unworthy? And there's more…isn't prayer usually asking for something? Go ahead, Dr. Dreyer.

Elizabeth Dreyer: For both of those questions and in the first question as well, I guess the only thing I would say is that to reduce prayer to a *quid pro quo* attitude is dangerous. I guess I would argue for the complexity of prayer, that what we are doing when we are asking for something is doing something about our own feelings, about our own experience, about who we think God is, but to set it up in terms of I do something and then that demands a response from God, feels literal to me. It feels reductive to me to think about prayer in those noncomplex ways.

Mary Collins: The way the question is framed makes for some jumps and assumptions that I think are not reflected in the wider prayer tradition. I'm reminded of what I think is the most powerful story that the Jewish Nobel prizewinner Elie Wiesel tells about himself and the time after his father died in the camp right before the liberation of Auschwitz. He tells how, on the anniversary of his father's death, when it was time for him to say the Kadish prayer of thanks to God for his father's life, he refused to do it because he was very angry with God about his father's death. Every year he remembered and every year he refused to say the prayer. And he was blaming God for the whole thing. But from the viewpoint of what I had said earlier, he never broke the relationship; to *refuse* to pray is to stay in relationship with God. I mean, you can be angry with God and God can take it. And, you know, in his case, he reports that he went on for more than forty years and then one year he was able to pray. Recently I saw an interview with him and he said that it began to dawn on him that to refuse to pray was to dishonor all of the people of his own family, to dishonor his father, and he began to see the whole set of relationships in a much bigger light. So again the question is, what's the deadline for coming to insight and saying that my prayer has been answered? It's much bigger and I think more mysterious and complex than yes/no and a clear formulation. I think when we are praying, we are really dealing with mystery.

Susan Calef: Just one of the things I think I would add to that is, of course, when I was talking about Mark's Gospel, it's clear that the prayer of Jesus in Gethsemane is not answered in the sense that it is not answered as Jesus would like. His desire was to be spared this and that was unanswered, and Mark's answer to that was that it was not God's will. And there is another, just to build on what Mary is saying, there is a case (I believe it's in 2 Corinthians), where Paul reports that three times he had prayed to be freed of this angel of Satan—we're not quite sure what he means there, if it's an illness, perhaps—but in any case, he had prayed three times to be relieved of this and clearly his prayer was not answered in the way that he wanted it, but then he goes on to report and to say that in a sense he gets an answer…now how long it took to get to that answer…but it finally came to him that God's voice is saying to him, "My grace is enough for you." So an answer came at some point but an answer different than Paul would have liked.

Dianne Bergant: I would like to say something to that, too. An example, again, of the inadequacy of theological language. Just the idea of an "answer" suggests that there was a question, or suggests that there was a petition, and that is only one kind of prayer. What kind of an answer would you expect? I mean, granted there is a response, but the language itself is very limited, and, in a certain sense, limits to one kind of a prayer, and that is a prayer of petition, as the example was, Paul's is a prayer of petition. When you ask something, you hope you get what you ask, but that is one kind of prayer. But there are other kinds of prayer where one just sits, you know, entranced with the loved one, whether that loved one be God or one's spouse, or one's child, as Elizabeth was saying. What kind of ecstasy, or what kind of response does a grandparent expect from looking at the child or a parent looking at a child? So again, you know, our language is very limited. And that is not a criticism of the question. It's a very valid question, but just realize that, again, it is an example of how we are dealing with something that is so beyond us; it is one of those examples of how we don't understand what we are immersed in.

Richard Miller: The next question is for Abbot Gregory. Speak of how to do *lectio divina* during times of extreme suffering, as that presented in psalms of lament, Jeremiah, and in the Agony of the Garden.

Gregory Polan: It's not easy to give an answer to that because the experience of reading the Scriptures and, for example, moving through the Scriptures if you are praying with a particular psalm and some crisis comes up, do you go to another psalm or do you go to a lament? Maybe I could just use one experience from my own life. Not quite, I would say *suffering*, but just maybe a critical moment. I remember when I was elected Abbot. I had just finished eleven years in the administration of our seminary, and I thought I had paid my dues. I was slated to go and teach Old Testament at our college in Rome at San Anselmo and six weeks before that departure I was elected Abbot. And I just remember that for a period of a good three months, I was in shock. However, I remember, and I cannot tell you what I was doing for my *lectio divina*, but whatever it was when I left that *lectio divina* in the morning period, there was a genuine sense of sweetness that came from the Word of God. It was comfort. It was consolation. It was hope. It was strength. And it wasn't anything specifically that I chose. So I think that we may all have particular passages that have come to mean something to us in moments of difficulty or moments of crisis, or just a particular passage that we may have heard many, many times and then all of a sudden, in a particular context of life we hear it, and it means something very special to us. It is something to be able to go back to Augustine's expression with regard to the Word of God as being ever ancient and ever new, the Word of God continually says something new, enlightening, inspiring, and helpful to us. I am not sure if I am totally answering the question, but I would just say in a time of crisis or suffering, I am not sure if it is always wise to particularly go to a lament.

Mary Collins: Could I supplement that? There is also an idiom in the monastic tradition in terms of *lectio divina,* talking about the *lectio* of life, and I have seen this particularly in the elderly and those who are dealing with very serious illness, and so this is a testimony from what I have witnessed in others, that there is a point at which, if they in fact have been faithful to their *lectio,* there is no longer a text that they return to, in a sense they become the text and they become the prayer, and a whole different kind of thing happens. There is a transformation in the person and it really involves kind of entering into the life experience and somehow letting that become the prayer and letting their lives become the prayer. And that is a whole transformative step in the process, but I think it is really dependent upon the fact that the other praying has been going on, all the other *lectio* has been going on, and somehow this transformation takes place.

Richard Miller: This question is for Dr. Calef. Connect for me the quote, "Why have you forsaken me?" with "Thy will be done."

Susan Calef: OK. Well, certainly in Gethsemane, as I said this morning, Jesus articulates his own desire to be spared the suffering, dying, and rising that he had spoken of earlier, but clearly that the crisis of the flesh that I described there, through the power of prayer, and in articulating his desire to the Father, he then moves on to be able to say, "Your will be done." And the Jesus of Mark's Gospel is presented as truly the man of faith, of trust, of confidence in God. The disciples, by contrast, are fearful and at times lack faith. So he comes through that Gethsemane scene with that crisis of flesh that was about fear of the pain, the vulnerability of the flesh, and so forth, still trusting in the good will of the Father, and so he can say, "Your will be done" in assent. But of course, as I mentioned, that does not exempt him from the real struggle on the cross. He can have submitted to that will, but the total aloneness, that sense of the remoteness, is still there for him. But as I look at the two scenes, what really strikes me now, the more I have spent time with it, is in that second cry on the cross, just because he has assented to the will of God, in some sense doesn't make the remoteness that he goes through there any easier. But he does…I would want to add, and I don't know if I said this today, I do not hear his cry as a cry of despair. Some people like to read that cry on the cross as a movement from real complaint to eventual confidence and praise as in Psalm 22. Some people find Jesus' statement on the cross very difficult and almost scandalous—that Jesus would talk this way to the Father. (And they try to soften that by saying, "Well, but that's Psalm 22 and it really means that he is feeling the comfort.") I don't think that is the way Mark intends it. He really wants us to see that even with the assent to the will of God, Jesus experiences profound distress at the darkness, the remoteness, but it is not despair—because he still cries out to God in prayer. So the trust in some sense is still there, but it is anguished.

Richard Miller: This question is for Sr. Bergant and Abbot Gregory, if you'd like, you can add your bit. Why is our prayer so far removed from that of the Old Testament?

Dianne Bergant: Part of it is a liturgical decision. Unfortunately, and I hope I don't sound like I'm blaming the liturgists, for most people, the exposure to the Scriptures is what they hear in liturgy, and the responsorial psalms seldom, if ever, have meaning in themselves in the liturgy. They are intended—and this is not a criticism here—to be a response to something in the first reading and sometimes all it is, is a word. Therefore, the average person is not exposed to laments. They may know some laments, or at least they may know passages from some laments, like "Have mercy on me, O God, in the greatness of your compassion, wipe out my offense." You know, the *Miserere*. Or they may know a little bit of *de Profundis:* "Out of the depths I cry to you, o Lord." They may know tidbits of this; they may know it because they've seen it, you know, on either a calendar or on an Argus poster, or they have seen it sometime during Lent because these phrases are very significant during Lent, as we think Lent is supposed to be a preparation. (No, that's not what the readings of Lent are. They speak about the goodness of God, but that's another workshop.) But the average person is not exposed to a lament. Some verses, perhaps, but not a lament.

Second, in terms of spirituality, I really don't know when in our history (maybe Elizabeth can answer this) we came to the sense that our spirituality has got to be anesthetized, that it cannot be that—somehow or other—we have to be willing to suffer. Now, I hope that we reach a point where we are willing to suffer, but that is not where the average person starts. And then we feel guilty because we're not there yet. We're not where the holy picture says that the saints were. I can't believe they started there either. So I think there is a kind of spirituality—but we certainly have really gotten a hold of it or it has gotten a hold of us—where we think that to complain to God is not religious. I want to say it is at least the first step to good religion. Now, if we don't move any further than that, then I don't think it's good religion, but you know, that might be an answer. So in a certain sense, it is because we are not exposed to it, and then, in addition, that we have been given a kind of spirituality that we have to be above it. Well, we're not above it.

Gregory Polan: I would agree with that, and maybe add one more dimension to it. Somewhere along the line we have also been taught that such kind of talk is probably blasphemy—"you don't talk to God that way"—and as a result, our prayer has become very antiseptic. I think also one of the other things that we have been so afraid to look at is the element of cursing in the psalms. And, of course, we all feel a certain level of being uncomfortable with that; but one of the interesting things about the psalmists is that there is cursing in the psalms, the psalmist is asking God to do this. He is not looking at himself to do this.

Susan Calef: I just wanted to add one other thing, because I share Dr. Bergant's concern about the lack of lament among us. We really didn't plan to get off on that together—in fact, we were laughing about sometimes you come to, you're on a program like this and it's like a conspiracy of the Spirit—the Spirit was just working among us. I only found out a couple of days before I came here that Dr. Bergant was going to focus on lament, which worked perfectly for me, who was heading toward lament in Mark. But one of the things I think is important about a speech form, a prayer form like a lament, is that it can have potential social consequences, and the *lack* of lament also has social consequences. Because if we are always praising and giving thanks, those are forms of speech that reinforce the *status quo*, "yes, this is fine, this is good." Whereas the lament, of course, because it's a protest—and think about those of us, I mean I lived through the '60s and whatnot—what protest *does*. Protest is the basis for eventually perhaps bringing about change in the social order; so I think for a community to be just yes-women and yes-men who only praise and give thanks, is problematic for the community, especially in our Christian tradition where we are concerned to deal with issues of social justice. We have to attend to the voices of the underside, and those who have reason to lament among us, because that lamentation can motivate us and move us to realize that we, who are the Body of Christ, must in some sense also respond. That is one of the other reasons I think it is important to look at recovering the lament in our communal liturgical prayer.

It should have some kind of a role. I don't know where we lost it, but I think there are all sorts of social functions that go with this.

Dianne Bergant: I heard you say we shouldn't become whiners though. I mean, we're not suggesting that.

Mary Collins: In terms of this history, there is some recognition that in the whole liturgical tradition there was a sense—at least in theological development—the resurrection of Jesus has taken care of everything. So you know we don't have to deal with this human thing anymore, and it really is a lack of faith if we are still lamenting. One of the ironies, I think, of the recent liturgical reform, and it really does say something about a kind of loss of nerve or loss of spirituality, in the Liturgy of the Hours, the whole 150 psalms have been prayed in a cycle and they are prayed in the monastery and in the diocesan priesthood, is when the Liturgy of the Hours for the Roman Rite was revised after the Second Vatican Council, the three cursing psalms were dropped. Now it's the first time in the history of the Roman Church that they only prayed 147 psalms and not a whole 150, which is a very strange commentary on "all Scripture is inspired," you know, for the good of the Church. I think most monasteries have kept the cursing psalms, and maybe it's because we live so close to each other that we need from time to time to say what we want to say in prayer.

Gregory Polan: I would just say also we pray all 150 psalms, so we do the cursing. But one of the things that I distinctly remember, and this may be a name that a number of you remember, probably 15 to 20 years ago, Father Carroll Stuhlmueller was at Conception Abbey and giving us some talks on the psalms, and the question was posed to him: "How do you pray the cursing psalms?" And he very succinctly—but I think astutely—said, "If we can't pray them in our own heart, then what we need to do is to pray them in solidarity with those many people around the world who cannot even voice their hurt, their grief, their anger, and their sadness." That has always been a memory that has stuck with me with regard to the cursing psalms.

Elizabeth Dreyer: Another area that strikes me as relevant is psychological. We are talking about a loss of nerve; I feel like we are insecure as pray-ers and therefore don't have the confidence in the relationship to "let it rip" with a curse or a lament. And what I call *construct living,* is that we get our ideas from prayer from all these people, but they "don't take." Imagine losing a child and not screaming a lament. And so it strikes me when we don't do the lament, it means that we're really not engaged.

Susan Calef: And just to follow up on that. With the psychological, Walter Brueggermann, the Old Testament scholar, when speaking on this costly loss of lament, points out that in some sense when we have terrible hurt, we all know from talk therapy that one of the ways to proceed is to get the pain out, tell the tough stuff, so that we can gradually get free of it. It is when it is held inside that it eats at us. And he points out that in some ways, the lament psalms are also very important that way because there is the opportunity, this cathartic effect, that when there is the pain it has to be expressed, articulated, and dealt with so that we can get beyond it and eventually go on. Healing takes place, and we can indeed give thanks for that and praise for that and so forth. But we need to be able to articulate the pain and can do that in this wonderful prayer form. And Israel knew that.

Raymond Boland: I just wanted to mention that in Celtic spirituality —and not in the New Age version—there is still a healthy respect for cursing in some of the prayers. The one that comes to mind immediately is the one that says something like, "God take care of our friends and bless them, and identify our enemies by making them lame so we'll know them by their limping."

Mary Collins: This is obviously a rich vein, but I had Walter Brueggermann as a professor and so much of what he taught us is seared into my brain forever. But one of the things that he talked about was this beautiful prayer *Kyrie eleison,* with which we begin our liturgy. How do we live that out? We should be tearing our clothes and pulling our hair out at the beginning of liturgy. And my question here is not just lamenting in terms of a fifteen-year-old killed in a car crash in a parish, but also in response to this pederasty thing, how have we torn our hair as a Church? What do we do liturgically?

Richard Miller: Any responses to that? One of the questions here asks about using the lament at a funeral service.

Dianne Bergant: I think that what it also calls for is some creativity liturgically, because, again, any liturgist knows there are some soft spots in the liturgy where you can work things in. But what it takes is insight and imagination in the local Church. And if you really believe that the only thing that needs to be done is to turn all the pages in a book, so that once we've said all the words that are in the book we have completed the liturgy, but have done it without any imagination or insight, I think we've had an empty liturgy. I think the other thing, though, is that imagination says that the Sunday liturgy isn't the only day we have experienced, as we see all over the country, how after a tragedy people will create shrines and have spontaneous events and soon, they seem most often to happen outside the Church because we lack so much imagination in terms of welcoming people to come and gather in the Church, so I think there is a lot to be done. Go ahead, Gregory, you look like you have an insight.

Gregory Polan: When 9/11 happened, we got on the radio in northwest Missouri and invited people to come to the Abbey to just pray, and we had a prayer service followed by an opportunity for people to just be together and to have some refreshments and the like. Our prayer service took probably about 45 minutes; people stayed to be together for almost three hours after that.

Dianne Bergant: You mentioned lament and what to do with it in terms of a funeral. The one thing that comes to mind, just again based on experience, my nieces were young teenagers when they lost their father to suicide, which of course, was very difficult. And I will never forget the church in Omaha where we had the service. I remember distinctly the reactions of my nieces because they wanted one of these canned wake services, you know, that's got the little bulletin all printed up and they make sure they grab them out of your hands as you're leaving. But it was the particular psalms that were used that night that were absolutely God-awful. I will never forget my nieces' reactions, and they were at an age where they had some issues about being part of the institutional Church, and I remember listening to what they had chosen for this service. There wasn't even a thought that maybe, you know, when you have a death such as this, maybe we need to really do something a little bit different, liturgically. So as soon as you mentioned lament, and although I am clearly somebody who thinks we need to be looking at how to use lament appropriately, I do not know that just any funeral is the place to do that. I think sometimes major calamities like 9/11 might require a time for us to express the anger and the protest. That night we were grinding bones into the dust and whatnot, and my nieces were quite frankly horrified. I mean, they were in deep grief, as were we all, and yet this was the service.

Richard Miller: The actual question, I've just found it here among the note cards: How would you structure complaint, trust, gratitude, and praise into a funeral service?

Mary Collins: If I might observe, they're all there already. The question is how do we actually *celebrate* them; what do we do to bring them *forward*? How do we bring that out? It can be brought out musically, it can be brought out in terms of a homily, it can be brought out in a whole variety of ways, but it really depends on the imagination of those who are exercising that liturgical ministry. One of the things we have to deal with at the present time—and this comes with the whole question of fear and the current state of the Church we're in and the fear of the imagination—is a problem with recent clergy formation that has resulted in a kind of resistance or inability in the young men who have been ordained more recently. They have been taught that liturgy is what's in the book. So you've got this conflict between what's authorized if it's not in the book, and I really do think it isn't a matter of what's the text in the book. Those things are there, but if they're not in the hearts of the assembly and they're not in the imaginations of the people, they have a hard time being brought out. So I think that the problem is really an impoverished understanding of liturgy, impoverished liturgical imagination, and fearful pastoral leadership at the present time. All of this conspires against us, and I think that my sense in listening to the discussions today is that the praying that we who are the Church are doing has to give us a fuller spirit that we can bring out into the Church instead of "why don't *they* help us do this?" We are the *they*, and I think the transformation has to start in us. We need to understand there is no way we can go forward in liturgy without doing these things. But as long as we have suppressed it in ourselves, it won't come out.

Raymond Boland: There's no doubt in my mind that if you're creative with liturgy, you can still exist within all of the rules that we're given and come up with a selection in readings and music, the comments, the homilist, and so forth that will give the aura to the liturgy that fills all the needs that were expressed. Just a few things, going back. At 12:00 the day of 9/11, we had a spontaneous liturgy and I was fortunate enough to be able to get around the barriers because every building in that place that had any government connection was being protected, and get back to the church and do it. I remember writing on the back of an envelope, literally, a few thoughts going out there and I have no idea what I said at this particular stage, other than the fact that we don't understand the horror going on and pray for those who have lost their loved ones. And then I just suggested that when you finish your prayers here in the church, please go home and hug your loved ones and appreciate the value of life and those who lost it that day. Apparently it was quite effective because I am an enemy of these canned prayers, you know. I can see why priests have to use them because sometimes they're burying people they've never met before or seen and so it's anonymous, it's difficult.

Richard Miller: This is for Sr. Collins, but I open it up to the rest of you as well. Could you sketch for us what it means to participate in the liturgy in a full, conscious, and active way? And I think the "full, conscious, and active way" is a quote from your talk.

Mary Collins: The "full, conscious, and active way" of participation are words from the Constitution on the Sacred Liturgy, and there has been a lot of discussion about what they mean. Certainly in terms of *full, active, conscious,* really talking about, first of all, exercising one's ministry. So if my ministry is to be part of the assembly, then it has to do with participating fully in the ministry of the assembly. Sometimes the ministry of the assembly is listening, sometimes it is singing, sometimes it is responding dialogically, but always, I think the ministry of the assembly is also responding interiorly. To be actively participating in the mystery is also to be participating in a contemplative way. I think that if you have a particular ministry, if your ministry is to be a reader, then the full participation in that ministry is, in fact, to prepare, to meditate on the text ahead of time, to be concerned about actually so proclaiming the Word that the people who are gathered understand it and hear it. I mean, whatever you are asked to do, whatever you role is, to do it with as much skill but also spiritual maturity and interiority, as you are capable of. And so in some ways I do not think it is a hard question to answer; it's a matter of some kind of *growing into* what is being asked of you. My refusal or decision not to sing, to stand like a lump, to decide that I don't want to—I don't know, extend the greeting of peace to other people and so forth—those are all failures to minister to other members of the assembly. Now sometimes, you know, the other side of it is that maybe the best I can do is be a lump, but then to let others minister to me so that I can listen to the Word and try as best I can. I think that language is not nearly so mysterious as it seems. I think if you really get down to it, it's to say, "What is my ministry, what is my role in this assembly, and how do I do it with skill, with insight, and with some kind of spirituality?"

Elizabeth Dreyer: I might add a quick story. In this introduction to religion course that I teach, I require students to attend a ritual—you know, as scholars—and we talk about preparing and how it's different from going just to pray. I ask them not to take notes during the ritual but to catch it as soon as they can afterward. And two things invariably happen—this is a coincidence of opposites. One is that many of them are going into church for the first time in nine or ten years, thinking about what is happening and how to analyze it in a scholarly way. The refrain that discourages me is that they feel like everyone in the church is a robot. They report over and over that there is nothing in anyone's face, there is nothing in anyone's body language to invite them to see life there. The one exception, a young woman who was a junior, went in and had a very powerful experience. She had gone to church every Sunday of her life since she was born and realized that she had judged everybody in church because they were all lumps, automatically presuming that there was nothing going on and at this one liturgy that she is doing this assignment for, she realized that she had judged them and she had no idea what was in their hearts. And she was repenting in this paper of her judgments of people. So I think again the both/and—you have to keep both sides going—begs us to ask the question about the inside *and* the outside. If there is something going on, on the inside, shouldn't it show somehow? Sometimes?

Richard Miller: This question is for Dr. Dreyer and Dr. Calef, I believe. This morning we heard that we *learned* to pray. This afternoon we learned that we should pay attention to the prayer that emerges. It seems contradictory to me. Would these two speakers like to expand on or clarify this? So the opposite or the tensions that we are told we have to learn to pray but that we should pay attention to prayer that emerges, and how we hold that together or deal with that.

Susan Calef: Well, I'm all for the idea of "both/and." I think I did say that we need to learn to pray, but I don't think that excludes what Dr. Dreyer was talking about. I think one of things that we learn through life as our spirituality develops is that we are exposed to different ways of praying by various people. There are lots of ways we can learn how to center ourselves and be more present to what is really about a love relationship. The more I look at love, both in Mark's Gospel and even in John's, I find myself thinking about the covenant relationship with God as very similar to the covenant relationship, for example, between two married people, where you would hope that as the trust is very strong, they share fully what they really feel and need and are going to bring even their worst selves to one another and share that. I think of the life of prayer as involving a kind of a learning to do that and learning to grow in trust. That's also why I think it's important to try and find ways of praying, because if we don't…it's like a marriage where people don't spend time together, the relationship slowly starts to die. You have to come together, which is a point that I know Dr. Collins made at a certain point: where is the relationship if we never come together? Whenever my students talk to me about prayer and what they are doing, I encourage them to try various ways of prayer. I share with them what has worked for me, but it is also about what bubbles up from inside, so I think, you know, the point you made earlier about both/and is very true.

Elizabeth Dreyer: Two things I would say. One is that the integrating element is *me*. The one who prays can learn techniques of how to pray and that affects watching and waiting to see what prayer emerges, and watching to see what prayer emerges can lead me to learn and desire other techniques of prayer. So I think the integration is the person. This is the same point in a different way. I think the tradition, the language of the tradition, is obviously coming out of discoveries. That's what I meant about Saint Catherine. She didn't read this in a book; she lived this and then wrote about it, and one of the blessings is that we have this tradition. One of the liabilities is that we take it as a prescription, and I think the insight of this kind of paradox comes from you and me and our experience, so that you can't exactly tell a person *how*. But talking about it like we're doing gives us the imagination. I mean, I am so grateful that I have the idea that maybe I could go that way, and so if I read somebody who has gone that way because he or she had the experience, it allows me the possibility of going that way because now it's in my imagination that this could happen to me.

Dianne Bergant: I think it's important to realize that as we've been talking about prayer today, we have really been talking about part of the range of tradition, but there certainly are lots of devotional prayers that we haven't talked about that are really part of the tradition. I see one of the things that is happening now as a kind of a resurgence on the part of people wanting to reclaim that. There is a tension, I think, sometimes, of oh, that's not a good way to pray, this is a better way to pray. And I think that it really does fit within this question of "pray the way you can," and don't disparage some part of an authentic part of the tradition. I remember an undergraduate student once who had completed an assignment. When I had asked her how she had done, she said she had done her assignment on the rosary, and she said, "I discovered the rosary is a prayer, not a string of beads." Well, you know, she had been deprived for a long time and I think we have to be very, very careful that when we say "pray the way you can and not the way you can't" that we make room for devotional prayer when that is the way people can pray.

Richard Miller: This is for Sr. Collins. The questioner says that you said, "Liturgy is effective if it is not offensive." When women are excluded in language, symbol, roles, that is very offensive. Is this really holy, effective liturgy?

Mary Collins: I was shown the question ahead of time and I don't recognize that I said that. I may have said whatever I said mumbling so it didn't come across. Good liturgy should stretch us. The crucifixion should offend us. The fact that so many things have actually moved into the liturgical life while the theologians are still debating them—as I said, there are women ministering, there are women reading, there is a gender-inclusive language in many, many places. Now I don't know about your parish, but if it isn't happening in your parish you've got to ask yourselves why it isn't happening. You're the ones doing the reading.

Elizabeth Dreyer: You know, one comment I would make on this very issue is the importance of prayer. It seems to be an absolute prerequisite to deal with the situation. Again, my experience of the young people is that it's a non-issue. I can't even get them to discuss it because they can't even imagine anybody who doesn't want women in leadership; anybody who doesn't think that women should be in leadership in the Church, they think they're nuts. They don't even engage it. It's just like, "Whoa, what's that about?" It's interesting to me. They've gone way beyond that. And society has gone beyond it.

Richard Miller: This is the last question. Are there any practical suggestions for overcoming dryness of prayer besides just "gutsing it out?"

Susan Calef: The one concrete essay that I referred to was Constance Fitzgerald's article, which is quite complex and I don't think I can spell it out simply here. I think showing up, deciding to just be there. But what Constance Fitzgerald suggests is moving to the right side of the brain activity and dealing with the dark night in a creative, imaginative way that engages things that we don't generally think of in our spiritual lives. So that is one very concrete explanation or alternative to just "gutsing it out." I guess another way of talking about "gutsing it out" is to remain faithful, to *choose* to remain faithful, to be in relationship, to stay in relationship.

Elizabeth Dreyer: Again, I think also sometimes the language betrays us. What does "dryness in prayer" mean? The impression or the implication is everything ought to be exciting. Does anybody live where everything is exciting? I mean, you know sometimes life is exciting. I would presume sometimes marriage is exciting and sometimes it's not. So I think the kinds of answers we give, the kinds of questions we ask, the implications or presuppositions I think we should ask ourselves are what image of God is behind this? How do

I understand God? Again, I'm not finding fault with the question because I use that same kind of language as well, so I'm not finding fault with the question or the questioner, but it presumes something about prayer and what our relationship with God should be, which presumes something about what God should be, which in a certain sense almost sounds like honeymoon language. Now, I'm celibate and I've never been married so I don't know what honeymoon is, but those of you who have had one…this is a rhetorical question and I don't want a show of hands…how long has it lasted? I mean, does it last all the time? Is that not something…are we not talking about the ebb and flow of the reality of life? So in a certain sense, without minimizing the importance of the question, one might ask, "What do you do when life is boring?" We don't normally end it, so what do we do? And we don't normally just tough it out. I mean, in a very real sense, if prayer is really very much a part of the way we interact with the reality of God or the reality of life in a certain sense, what do you do if things are going in a way that is exciting, or when you are just overwhelmed? We don't turn part of our brain off, you know, when we get into religious area, we've got the same kind of equipment that we use when we talk about one another and we talk about God because it's the same person that's reacting, the same person that is searching. So again, I don't like the idea when I feel that any kind of relationship I have really doesn't enrich me, and there are times when I feel they don't—and they are not refreshing, and there are times when I feel they don't—and I know there are times when I'm not! And that is part of life. So the question is "What do we do in those times?" And I would ask all of us, particularly the person who asked the question, "What do you do when *life* is like that?" And I suggest that, in a certain sense, learn from life of how you should respond in your relationship with God, as well. Unfortunately, it's part of life and it may be not that God is not exciting, it's that we're not, this is a bad day and consequently with whomever I interact, it is not going to be exciting.

Appendix I

A Sampling of Written Questions Presented at the Symposium

1. How do we reconcile "complaint to God" with not blaming God for bad things?
2. Why is it not a common practice anymore to begin prayer with the Sign of the Cross?
3. What does it mean to say prayers are "unanswered"; that they are not "worthy"; that God heard but answered "no"; or, that the "prayer" is unworthy?
4. If we ask for something in prayer, can our prayers manipulate God?
5. Are there any practical suggestions to overcoming "dryness" in prayer?
6. How does sin affect your prayer relationship with God? Does it cut off the grace that comes through prayer?
7. We had excellent presentations on the methods of prayer in sacred Scripture and tradition. Speak of the effects of prayer. How does prayer change the present or future?
8. What does it mean "to participate in the liturgy in a full and conscious and active way?
9. How would you structure complaint, trust, gratitude, and praise into a funeral service?
10. Do we (individually or communally) avoid grief because we cannot explain it? Or, do we demand this explanation of our priests, who in turn feel inadequate to the task?
11. Comment on the events of nature (flowers, mountains as in the psalms) to lift our spirits to God.
12. How does changing words in the communal liturgy affect the union within the Church? Can this be more divisive?
13. "Liturgy is effective if is not offensive." When women are excluded in language, symbols, and some roles, this is offensive. Does this affect the holiness and effectiveness of the liturgy?

14. Speak to how to do *Lectio Divina* during times of extreme suffering, as presented in the lamentation psalm, Jeremiah, or the agony in the garden.

15. What practical suggestions for liturgy do you have for incorporating grief and lamentation into the official prayer of the Church?

16. How can you get *Lectio Divina* started in a parish?

17. How do you choose an appropriate Scripture reading for *lectio,* or do all of them work?

18. Where does the gift of healing prayer fit in Catholic theology?

19. Can the Holy Spirit use laity to heal physically through prayer?

20. Does the "evangelism movement" emphasize Jesus as Lord to the neglect of God as Father? Do you feel there is a diminished recognition of God as Father?

21. How do we get over the stigma of being poor in America?

22. People often come to church for baptism, first Communion, confirmation and marriage. What causes this? How can this be changed?

23. In prayer, as we try to trust in God's plan, how do we gather together and grasp together the pain of the local church when there is so much pain and confusion? How do we cry out alone? How do we form community in the midst of darkness?

24. What is the role of prophets today? Who are the prophets today?

25. What is the difference between centering prayer and contemplation?

26. Have the GRIM and the new translation of the Roman Missal helped or hindered the development of the communal nature of the liturgy?

27. How could the Church make the most of the opportunity presented by the new Roman Missal?

28. Is "Trinity" a Christian concept or a Catholic concept?

Appendix II

Speakers' Biographies

Dianne Bergant, C.S.A.

Sr. Dianne Bergant is a member of the Congregation of St. Agnes and Professor of Biblical Studies and Director of the Doctor of Ministry Program at Catholic Theological Union in Chicago. She began her theology studies at Marquette University and then took her M.A. and Ph.D at Saint Louis University. Sr. Dianne's list of publications runs several pages, including scholarly as well as popular titles. Her Sunday scripture columns in *America* have been widely admired.

Susan A. Calef, Ph.D.

Susan Calef began her academic career at Marymount College in Tarrytown, New York, with an M.A. in Philosophy and Religious Studies. She took a second M.A. in Biblical Studies at Notre Dame, followed by her Ph.D in Biblical Literature and Languages there. Presently, Dr. Calef is Assistant Professor and Director of Graduates Studies in Theology at Creighton University. She has received numerous awards and fellowships for her excellence in teaching. Among her published critical reviews and conference papers, the most interesting title that jumps out is *By Grit and Grace: Women of the Early Christian Frontier.*

Very Reverend Gregory Polan, O.S.B.

Abbot Gregory has been abbot at Conception Abbey since 1996, where he also teaches Scripture at the Seminary College. Among his degrees are a Ph.D in Theology and an S.T.D. in Biblical Theology at the University of Ottawa. Abbot Gregory has written many books and articles, and he also has given many retreats and conferences. Abbot Gregory plays the organ and is a composer. He is on the editorial board of *The Bible Today*. In the Diocese of Kansas City-St. Joseph, he is the diocesan representative for ecumenical and interreligious affairs.

Mary Collins, O.S.B.

Sr. Mary Collins has a distinguished background as a Professor of Liturgy at The Catholic University of America for many years. She has written and lectured widely on liturgy and spirituality. Sr. Collins was prioress at the Benedictine Monastery of Mount St. Scholastica in Atchinson, Kansas, from 1999–2005. She received the Notre Dame University's Michael Mathis Award for significant contributions to liturgical life in the United States.

Elizabeth A. Dreyer, Ph.D.

Elizabeth Dreyer is Professor of Religious Studies at Fairfield University. She received her Ph.D from Marquette University. Her focus of teaching is the wisdom of the Christian mystical tradition. In 2004, she received the Elizabeth Ann Seton Medal from the College of Mount St. Joseph in Cincinnati for her outstanding contributions to Catholic theology in the United States. Among her seven books is the title *The Cross in Christian Tradition: From Paul to Bonaventure.* Dr. Dreyer's breadth of expertise from medieval theology and mysticism nourishes contemporary lay spirituality.

Most Reverend Raymond J. Boland, D.D.

Bishop Boland was ordained Bishop of Birmingham in 1988 and came to Kansas City-St. Joseph in 1993 where he served as shepherd until 2005. He was educated in Ireland and ordained for the Archdiocese of Washington, D.C., where he led three parishes and held many administrative roles. His many national appointments included the Bishops' Communications Committee, the Nominations Committee, and the Pro-Life Committee. For years Bishop Boland was the leader of U.S. Catholic Conference Delegation to the Northern Ireland Inter-Church Committee.